The author, Harold Horsfall Hilton, in front of the Hoylake clubhouse after winning the 1897 British Open Championship.

The links of the Royal Liverpool Golf Club at Hoylake, the first hole.

Reprinted, 1998, by Ailsa, Inc.
ISBN: 0-940889-45-5

FLAGSTICK BOOKS

Edition of

MY GOLFING REMINISCENCES

By
Harold H. Hilton

Foreword by John E. Behrend

Publisher's Note

John Behrend, who contributed the Foreword, is a fine amateur golfer, a prolific author, a former Captain of The Royal and Ancient Golf Club of St. Andrews and of The Royal Liverpool Golf Club at Hoylake. A long-time member and present Trustee of Hoylake, he is one of those most responsible for maintaining it's position as England's premier golf club. He lives overlooking the Hoylake links.

We have added a chronology to this edition to place the succession of tournaments described in an easily referred to and clear historical context.

Robert S. Macdonald

Foreword
by
John E. Behrend

Avisitor to Hoylake, entering the main hall of the Royal Liverpool Golf Club, will quickly become aware of the "presence" of Harold Horsfall Hilton.

The first thing that catches the eye is the bronze head cast to honour his nomination to the World Golf Hall of Fame and presented to the club by that august body. His cap, one notices, is on the back of his head with a fringe of hair showing - the turn of the century Jasper Parnevik look. Then there is a small oil painting of him by J.T. Inglis, full of colour and action, against a background of the Dee's estuary. There are six Michael Brown prints displayed in the hall and he features in five of them. In the two showcases there are many of his medals, including the two he won for his Open Championship victories. There are also six of his Amateur Championship medals (four gold and two of his three silver ones); and another marking his United States Amateur win, not to mention fifty or so of the scratch medals he won at his many different clubs. He is there again, looking down from the halflanding, that famous Hilton portrait painted in 1913 by R. Jack. It hangs between the ones of Bobby Jones and Johnny Ball, the only three amateur golfers to have won the Open Championship, six times between them. Hilton's second Open victory was at Hoylake, the first to be staged there, one hundred years ago. This then is a good time to remind ourselves of Hilton's golfing achievements, and there is no better way of doing it than by reading about them in "My Golfing Reminiscences".

One of his earliest memories was, as a ten-year-old, winning the 1879 Boys Medal at Hoylake, a competition for youngsters under the age of sixteen. It is strange to think of a ten-year-old having a caddy, but he did and it was Joe Lloyd, a local man, who later became professional at Pau in the south of France during the winter months and at the Essex County Country Club near New York in the summer. In 1897 Joe Lloyd played in and won the United States Open Championship, which, in retrospect, created a remarkable double for Hoylake (Hilton won the British Open there in the same year as Lloyd), although, at the time, winning the U.S. Open was no big deal. It was over thirty-six holes then and it took Francis Quimet in 1913, when he beat Vardon and Ray in the play-off, to make the British take note of it.

Hilton, as is generally known, became the first editor of "Golf Monthly" in 1911 and two years later the editor of "Golf Illustrated". Before then he had contributed instructional chapters in a number of books, including Horace Hutchinson's "The Book of Golf and Golfers" and John Low's "Concerning Golf", but he had started writing even earlier, contributing a weekly article of some 2000 words of entertaining stuff for the Sporting Chronicle, much of it about the Merseyside clubs and written in a plain and easy style. The first of these to be pasted into the Royal Liverpool Club scrapbooks is dated 4th January 1898 and at the end of this first column is a paragraph about the state of the links at Hoylake. It was, as he wrote, covered in "soil and manure" and he concluded the paragraph with, "nature is all very well in her way, but occasionally she requires a little artificial aid". What could be simpler. This is the style in which "Reminiscences" is written.

The book was published in 1907, having been put together during the two preceding years. It tells the story only up to 1904, and that is barely half of it. Between 1904 and 1909 he had his five barren years with no Amateur medals and no success in the Open. In 1910 he began to show signs of recovery, reaching the semi-final of the Amateur Champion at Westward Ho! 1911 was his greatest year. He won the Amateur at Prestwick, defeating each of his first four opponents on the thirteenth green. His quarter-final game went to the sixteenth and that was the closest match. E.A. Lassen lost to him in the final by 4 and 3. A few weeks later, down at Sandwich, he was leading the field with seven holes to play in the Open Championship, having over-taken Vardon, Herd, Taylor and Braid all of whom had started the final round ahead of him. A mishap at the twelfth, where he bunkered his drive and missed a short putt to take 6, broke his concentra-tion, and a 5 at the short sixteenth ended his chances. He finished tied for third, one shot behind Vardon and Massy who contested a play-off. Next came his victory in the United States Amateur at Apawamis. First he won the medal for the qualifying competition and then he played through the match-play stages without much difficulty until he came to the final against Fred Herreshoff. This was a pulsating affair with Hilton losing a lead of six up with thirteen to play, before benefiting from a lucky bounce to win at the thirty-seventh hole. In 1913 he won the amateur Championship for the forth time. There would have been plenty to write about in a second volume of "Reminiscences".

Hilton was still competing in championships after the war and in 1927 both he and Johnny Ball competed on their home links with the opportunity of achieving a record one hundred wins in Amateur Championship matches. Both lost in the early rounds. Inevitably comparisons of the two great pre-war amateur golfers have been drawn. They were so different. Ball's swing was, according to Darwin, a thing of beauty, poised and rhythmic. Hilton, who was six years younger and smaller in stature, generated his power by means of a swing noted more for its energy that its elegance. They were set apart in other ways. Ball was Hoylake's favourite hero worshiped by the locals. He was the first to bring fame to Hoylake and his placid and unassuming demeanor was more appealing to Victorian sentiment than was the self-confident air, cigarette, white shoes and jaunty walk of Hilton, an image which may have sprung from the Spy cartoon. It was not a worthy one. He was kind, fair-minded, never complaining and always willing to help others. As to his own golf, the word assiduous seems the appropriate one. He practiced and experimented for hours, finally, unlocking the game's secrets, or at least some of those that were relevant to himself. Bernard Darwin said of him "there are just a few people in the world who really know a subject; he knew golf"... and on the links he applied that knowledge with the three H's - hand, head and heart: Harold Horsfall Hilton.

Chronology

1744   The first organized golf club, The Honourable Company of Edinburgh Golfers, comes into existence.

1834   King William IV grants the St. Andrews Golf Club permission to call itself the Royal and Ancient Golf Club of St. Andrews.

1848   The gutta percha golf ball replaces the old feather ball.

1860   The first British Open Championship, played over thirty-six holes, held at Prestwick, is won by Willie Park of Musselburgh. Eight golfers in field.

1861   John Ball born in Hoylake, England.

1864   The first English Golf Club founded at Westward Ho!

1869   Harold Hilton born near Hoylake, England. The newly organized Liverpool Golf Club, destined to become the father of the British Amateur Championship, selects the links of Hoylake as its home.

1870	Harry Vardon born in Grouville on the channel island of Jersey.
1875	Hilton attends local school along with John Ball and other notable Hoylake golfers. Willie Park wins his fourth Open at Prestwick.
1877	At age eight Hilton first enters boys competition at Hoylake.
1878	Hilton wins under -12 Boys competition.
1879	Hilton wins under -16 Boys competition, has an 18 handicap. Jamie Anderson wins his third straight Open at St. Andrews. Forty-one golfers in field.
1880-1884	Hilton attends boarding school in Norfolk, England.
1884	Hilton is taught golf at Hoylake by Willie More.
1885	The Royal Liverpool Golf Club organizes the first Amateur Championship over its Hoylake links. John Ball loses to his father in third round. A.F. Macfie from St. Andrews beats Horace Hutchinson from Westward Ho! in finals.

1885-1886	Hilton's first job in commercial office, little golf played.
1887	Hilton enters Amateur at Hoylake for first time, loses to John Ball's father in third round. John Ball loses to Horace Hutchinson in finals 1 down. Willie Park Jr. wins Open at Prestwick.
1888	The St. Andrew's Golf Club, the first permanent golf club in the United States, formed in Yonkers, New York.
1889	Hilton's second appearance in Amateur at St. Andrews. Loses to Laidlay, eventual winner, in first round.
1890	John Ball becomes first amateur and first Englishman to win Open Championship, held at Prestwick. Also wins Amateur at Hoylake beating Hilton in fourth round. Hilton wins first Open tournament at North Berwick.
1891	Hilton loses in finals of Amateur at St. Andrews to Scottish rival Laidlay.
1892	Hilton wins Open Championship at Muirfield, first time event is 72 holes over two days. Loses 3 and 1 to John Ball in finals of Amateur at Sandwich.

1893   Hilton loses in first round to Freddie Tait in Amateur at Prestwick. Harry Vardon and J.H. Taylor play in Open for first time.

1894   Hilton loses again to Tait in fourth round of Amateur at Hoylake, won by John Ball. J.H. Taylor breaks through in Open at Sandwich, held outside Scotland for first time. The United States Golf Association formed.

1895   J.H. Taylor wins his second Open at St. Andrews. The first official United States Open and Amateur Championships held at Newport Golf Club, Newport, Rhode Island.

1896   Hilton loses to Tait for third time in finals of Amateur at Sandwich. Vardon wins first of six Opens at Muirfield, beating Taylor in playoff.

1897   Hilton wins his second Open at Hoylake, defeating James Braid by one stroke.

1898   Tait wins Amateur at Hoylake, eliminating Hilton for fourth time. Vardon wins Open at Prestwick, Hilton two strokes back.

1899	Tait defeats Hilton in Amateur for fifth time, won by John Ball. Vardon wins third Open at Sandwich. Boar War begins.
1900	After twelve attempts Hilton wins Amateur at Sandwich. (Tait is killed in Boar War and John Ball remains at front.) Vardon wins United States Open at Chicago Golf Club, Taylor second.
1901	Hilton wins his second Amateur title at St. Andrews. In the Open also at St. Andrews: Braid first, Vardon second, Taylor third, Hilton fourth. Death of Queen Victoria. Her son succeeds as Edward VII.
1902	Rubber-cored ball introduced. Winners of Open and Amateur, Herd and Hutchings, among very few who try new ball.
1903	Vardon wins his fourth Open at Prestwick by six strokes.
1904	First foreigner -- an American Walter J. Travis -- wins Amateur at Sandwich.

MY GOLFING
REMINISCENCES

BY

HAROLD H. HILTON

London

JAMES NISBET & CO., LIMITED

BERNERS STREET, W.

1907

MY GOLFING REMINISCENCES

CHAPTER I

"Where did you learn your golf?" is a question which I have often been asked, and I have generally evaded it by answering, "I began to play the game at Hoylake." But, candidly, it is not true to say that I learnt my game altogether at Hoylake, as I have been learning the game all my life; and what is more, I am still willing to learn, if I think I can see anything worth learning. A golfer's education is never finished; he certainly may forget a little of what he has learnt, but he can always pick up some simple wrinkle which may be of use to him in his after career.

Of course I certainly owe a great deal to my early golfing education at Hoylake—it was, so to speak, the nursery of my game—and, looking back at the players it has turned out, it is almost needless to say that an excellent nursery it must have been. I cannot quite say at what age I began to play the game, but I am assured of this, that when I commenced it must have been as a boy of very immature years; at the age of two I was taken to live in a house right on the very edge of the links; and as I was a boy with a natural predilection for athletics, it cannot have been long before I handled a club.

I am told that the first club I handled was one of my father's. This is more than probable, as in my youthful days I had the undesirable habit of making use of the goods of all my relations—not to mention the goods of those who were not my relations—and decking myself up in habiliments which did not belong to me. In consequence I earned the sobriquet of "Paddy"—a sobriquet which remained with me for many years.

Still, I have a distinct recollection of one of my first efforts. I remember well enough that I was attempting to use a club which was much too long for me, and holding it short, with the top of the shaft protruding past my left ear. The upward swing was quite easy, but in the downward swing there was a decided obstruction, as the club struck me on the left side of the head. On mature consideration this would seem to be the only possible result. Even in those infantile days, however, I was of an experimental turn of mind, and I decided to try to hit the ball with the top of the shaft protruding beyond my right ear. The result was not quite as painful, but it was even less effective, as I never even finished the upward swing, the handle of the club this time striking me on the right side of the head, and another valiant effort ended in nought.

Attempt number three was even more painful, but the physical pain passed me by and fell upon another small boy who was watching my vain efforts. This time it was not the club handle which caused the trouble, it was the club head, which struck him fairly on the temple. You see I had decided to hold the club at the extreme end, so as to save my own head; as it appeared to be the only possible solution of the difficulty. But that club had made up its mind to hurt some one seriously that day, and it certainly stuck to its initial resolution, as it left a very nasty wound, and, at the same time, a very vivid impression upon my mind that it is never safe to swing a club unless you are absolutely sure that there is no one immediately behind you. It was a lesson taught me early in life, and I have never forgotten it. Even the idea of the possibility of hitting any one in the backward swing puts me off my stroke, and I always prefer both my opponent and his caddie facing me, a position in which there is no danger.

Shortly after this I went to school—a school which has turned out more than one good golfer; when I first entered its portals as a boy of six, amongst the pupils were Johnnie Ball, Herbert Tweedie, and Herbert Farrar, not to mention several others, who might have made a name for themselves had they stuck to the game in later years. Mr. Arthur Turpin, the proprietor of the school, had also under his charge the late

Willie More — from a scientific point of view one of the finest golfers that ever lived — my younger brother Reggie, F. P. Crowther, jun., and H. P. Crowther; and notwithstanding that it was but a small day school, there can be few schools which have turned out a finer collection of amateur golfers.

In every walk of life a child or a man has ambitions; without them he is of little use to this world. My ambition has always been to conquer something in the game of golf. I began somewhat early in life. The first difficulty I tried to surmount was the feat of driving over the "Bowling Green"—it was a real bowling green, which belonged to the Green Lodge Hotel. It was probably not more than thirty yards wide; but everything in this world is a question of degree, and a carry of thirty yards is no mean effort for a boy of seven years of age. What made the occasion all the more trying was the fact that this green was surrounded by a fence, and, if the ball had landed inside, it would probably have

had to be retrieved when darkness had over-
spread the earth, as there was a fearsome notice
to the effect that trespassers would be prosecuted. On thinking the question over in
later years I have had my doubts as to whether
this intimation would have been carried out in
its legal entirety, but it sufficed for the infantile
mind. In consequence the attempted feat was
always approached with a certain amount of
trepidation.

Finally, after this was achieved the youthful Alexanders sighed for fresh fields to conquer, and on the way to school the only other
obstacle to overcome was the back garden of
the late Mr. Robert Wilson, otherwise called
"The Chieftain." This garden was probably no
wider than the bowling green, but it was surrounded by a belt of trees, and in consequence
was infinitely more difficult to surmount. Moreover, whilst the bowling green had a notice
—"Trespassers will be prosecuted," the Chieftain's garden owned a very large rain-tub, on
which was painted in very large white letters,
"Beware of the dog." Now there is a grave

distinction between the fact that you will be prosecuted and the fact that there is a dog present. The one suggests that there is a possibility of trouble in the future; the other does not trouble with the future—a dog only argues with the present. Again, in the first instance your parents are the ones who will probably suffer, whilst in the second they cannot bear the responsibility and pain if a dog really does bite you.

Therefore, every boy was very chary of attempting the Chieftain's garden unless he knew full well that he had an excellent chance of carrying it. By the way, in after years I found out that "Dan," the dog referred to in white letters, was not at all a fearsome animal; he had a small fat body and a large bark, and, when he did bark, preferred to discuss the situation some five or ten yards away. I have always thought that it would have been infinitely kinder had the Chieftain intimated this fact upon the rain-tub. It would have made life much easier for the children, and at the same time not have cost much in paint.

But these are merely childish days, though possibly days in which I was as keen upon the game of golf as ever I was in my life, and I have been very much interested in the game on several occasions during my career.

Now to the serious business of a competitive career. My first appearance was almost naturally in the boys' competition at Hoylake. I was eight years of age at the time. The competition was divided into two classes—the first being for all boys under sixteen years of age, who played the full eighteen holes, the second for boys under twelve years of age, and the course they had to play was only twelve holes. I entered for the major event, that is, the eighteen holes, though why I know not. In any case I failed, and that notwithstanding a very substantial handicap. In the following year discretion overcame my vaulting ambition, and, entering for the junior competition, I won the first prize from scratch. In the following year, at the age of ten, ambition once again came to the fore. I entered amongst the seniors, and had no cause to regret doing so, as I won

the scratch medal. I had been rather highly
honoured that day, for had not Joseph Lloyd,
the present professional at Pau, and at that
time the smartest caddie on the Hoylake links,
requested to be allowed to carry for me. It was
an honour which I did not thoroughly appreciate until thinking the situation over in after
years. The "General," as he was called, must
have been of great service to me, as in those
days I seldom played anything approaching a
full round, and knew literally nothing at all
about the distances, much less anything about
the rules. It is more than probable that he
played the game, and I simply struck the ball,
but in any case it was a very successful combination. In this competition I was given a
handicap of eighteen, and in consequence I
was easily first in the handicap results, but
could only take one prize. A peculiar feature
in this round was the fact that never during
the whole eighteen holes did I feel the slightest
sign of nervousness or anxiety, possibly owing to
the ignorance of childhood. The following year,
at the mature age of eleven, my nerve gave way

for the first time. I couldn't sleep the night
before the competition, and when playing I
was simply trembling with fright. I suppose I
had suddenly found a reputation, and the burden
was too big to carry. I did not win that medal,
being beaten by three strokes by W. E.
Whineray, with whom I happened to be playing.

From that time until the age of fifteen my
interest in the game of golf considerably waned,
no doubt because, being at a boarding-school, I
took a greater interest in other branches of
athletics. However, I managed to win the medal
in the three following years, all three on what
in racing parlance would be termed very hurried
preparations; in fact, one year I never struck a
shot on the links until I arrived on the tee,
and in consequence only just scrambled home
from a very poor field, and I should only have
met my due had I lost; indeed, I am more impressed in each succeeding year with the absolute
necessity of continuous practice.

It was during these years that Johnnie Ball
was making a name for himself as just about
the finest amateur golfer in the kingdom, and

he was naturally the idol of all the smaller
boys. My idolatry for his prowess had the painful effect of costing me one whole shilling
over his match with Douglas Rolland. At the
time I was at school in Norfolk, and it so
happened that there was one other boy at the
school who knew something about the game
of golf. He was a native of Musselburgh, and
occasionally we had little arguments about the
game. He used to quote Bob Fergusson and
other Scottish celebrities, and was quite im-
partial, but he could always find about six
Scotsmen who could beat any Englishman. I
had only one reply as to the prowess of his
many celebrities, and that was that Johnnie
Ball was quite good enough for me. One day
when we were looking through the *Field*
together, he suddenly remarked—" Hello, here
is a man going to play Ball," and on looking
at the paper I saw that it was Douglas Rolland.
I had never even heard of his name before, and
possibly spoke a little contemptuously of his
chance, and scorned the idea of any one beating Johnnie. Whatever it was I said, it evi-

dently aroused the ire of the Scotch boy, as he promptly remarked—" I will bet you a shilling that Rolland wins." I didn't hesitate a moment in accepting the offer, only thinking at the time that I hoped he had an honest and a good memory. When pay-day did come, however, it was I who had to disgorge. I couldn't make it out at all—I was simply dumfoundered at the result. I tried hard to forget the incident, but that boy Gibson would not let me. Eventually I had recourse to the extreme measure of wilfully avoiding him—I was getting really tired of the subject.

Before leaving the subject of the golfing days of my extreme youth, I may say that until the age of fifteen I received instruction from only one individual, and that was from my father. Not that I was at all anxious to accept these well-meant efforts to keep me along the straight and narrow pathway. I could not see the logic of a man with a handicap of twenty even suggesting that there could be a right and a wrong way of playing the game. I could even beat him myself, and it seemed ridiculous that he could teach me anything. Still he persevered very hard, and his perseverance has borne good fruit, as by his constant reiteration of the words, " Why don't you follow through ? " I was eventually induced to adopt this mode of procedure, even if it was only to keep him quiet. And it is certainly this principle of following through which has made my swing the true one that it is. I can always remember an example of what I then considered paternal censoriousness. To my youthful mind it appeared to me that he simply took advantage of the fact that he was my father to bully me. It was a spring morning, just at the time of the year when the morning air is decidedly cool. I was dragged out of bed about six. I say dragged out, as I literally was dragged out, and in those days I was not at all partial to getting up to see the sun rise. I arrived on the tee a very irritable boy, and I would not try to play the game. I simply slogged at the ball—a species of mild protest at the iniquitous outrage of being taken from my warm bed. Soon came the old, old cry, " Why don't you follow through ? " It was repeated so often that I eventually became a little sick of it, and when playing my second shot to the fifth hole, I took a flying run at the ball, and after hitting it, ran in the direction the ball had gone. " Is that following through ? " I remarked, feeling that I had scored quite a big point. The reply quite chastened my spirit : " Harold, if you are going to be a big baby, you had better go home." I had enough judgment to feel the good sense of the remark.

When I look back upon my career it is always impressed upon me that when I had attained the age of fifteen years my golfing education had barely commenced. I certainly had learnt to hit the ball, and hit it very truly, but I had not the faintest idea how I achieved the results. It was a game for which I had only two qualifications—first, a natural physical ability for games, and second, certain powers of imitation—powers which are invariably very marked in all children. I had never taken the trouble to watch other players, and see how they achieved their results—in my opinion absolutely the finest schooling in the world for a young player. When I was fifteen years of age, however, I was granted an opportunity of obtaining an insight into the many mysteries of the game, and for this insight I was mainly indebted to the late Willie More, to whom I have before alluded. At one time he was a member of the Royal Liverpool Club, but later in life he became professional at Chester and Johannesburg, a profession he adopted owing to a weakness in his lungs, and the consequent medical dictate that he must at any cost lead an open-air life. At the time I speak of he was between sixteen and seventeen years of age, but even at that age he knew more about the game than most men of twenty-five or even thirty. He treated the game as a science, and although he probably slightly overdid the subject in respect that he was too experimentally theoretic, still he achieved wonderful results, and I remember one day when he beat Johnnie Ball in two consecutive rounds. He couldn't drive within yards of John, but the latter was driving very wildly just then, and the tortoise beat the hare. It was up to the hole and on the green that More's strength lay.   He had half-a-dozen ways of playing every shot, and was particularly good when slicing a ball into the wind with a wooden club.   To the present generation his name may not even be known, but he accomplished two very good performances; the first being to reach the fifth round of the first championship at Hoylake in 1885, when he was beaten by the ultimate winner, Mr. Horace Hutchinson—not at all bad for a boy of seventeen; and again at St. Andrews in 1891, after he had turned professional, he finished fifth in the open championship.   At the tenth hole in the second round he had a very decided chance of winning, as at that point he was only one stroke behind Hugh Kirkaldy, the ultimate winner. Kirkaldy, who was playing in front of him, took five to the short hole, and Billy More saw him do it, and at the same time knew his score. In his anxiety to take every advantage of this mistake he tried for far too much, and found the right-hand bunker, took three to get out, and six to the hole.   This broke him up, as his temper, never of the most reliable quality, gave way.

How good he would have been, had his health been satisfactory, it is impossible to say, but he certainly was a beautiful golfer, and moreover was blessed with a wonderful nerve and any amount of pluck.

I have brought his name into this story, mainly on account of the fact that at this period of my life I had five consecutive months' golf with him, and he certainly taught me much of the scientific possibilities of the game. I cannot say that I followed all his little theoretical fads; he had far too many to take in all at once, and they had to be taken home, chewed, and digested, but they taught me much. First, I learnt the advantage of the overlapping or interlocking grip, particularly when playing short approaches. In the driving department of the game, I did not make too great a success of this overlapping grip, as my hands were too small to obtain a sufficiently powerful grip of the handle of the club, and finally I dropped it. My early experience of this grip is, however, still evident in the way I hold my club, the little finger of

B

my right hand always being off the handle of the club.

In these five months I came on by leaps and bounds. I began playing More with the odds of a third, then the odds came down to four strokes, and finally I played him on level terms, and held my own fairly well. Although I hardly touched a club for the next three years of my life, I always consider that I learnt more in those five months than I have ever learnt in any two other years of my golfing career.

It was about this time that I played my first game against Johnnie Ball. It was a foursome, in which I was partnered with More against Johnnie and Herbert Tweedie, and there was great joy in our camp when we beat them. Shortly after this I tackled John in a single ; he gave me a third and I won, and was consequently much elated. The smile was on the other side of my face on the next occasion, as he sent me home thinking very hard. It seemed to me as if it would have taken about a stroke a hole to bring us together.

It was just about this time that I obtained

my first experience of serious golf, as on top of these foursomes against Johnnie Ball I was backed for a wager against one of the scratch players of the club. I was not at all nervous in this match, as I had an idea I should win. I had nothing to lose and everything to gain, and moreover, shortly before the event, he had arrived on the course without a match, and asked me whether I would care to play. Naturally I was delighted. I shall always remember the remark he made to me at the tee on that occasion—"Well, I suppose, Harold, you are growing far too big a boy to receive strokes." I didn't receive any strokes, and I won on the seventeenth green. This gave me confidence in the "wager" match, and I once again won, this time on the sixteenth green.

Another vivid impression I retain in connection with that period was the occasion of a visit from John Laidlay to Hoylake ; we had all heard that the most famous Scottish amateur was to come down to play Johnnie, and our interest was great. The first part of the invasion we came across in the form of Laidlay's clubs,

which we saw being taken into Morris's shop, and
we followed in and inspected them. The result
of the inspection was not flattering to Scottish
club-makers, as the clubs seemed abnormally long
in the face and clumsy in appearance. From
my earliest recollection the club-heads turned
out from the shop of John Morris have always
been comparatively short in the face, and several
of us were in the habit of using what was
termed a wooden niblick, which was really the
forerunner of the brassie of the present day.
But if the inspection of the clubs proved unsatis-
factory, it was as nothing to our contemptuous
wonderment when we saw Laidlay's style. In
our youthful ignorance we came to the conclusion that no man who played in a style like
that could possibly be a good player, and as
Johnnie Ball simply walked all over him, there
seemed a certain amount of justice and truth
in our opinions.

But Johnnie Ball was at his best that day,
and after the match I am told that Laidlay
sorrowfully remarked—" What is the good of
bringing me down to play a machine?"   I

may say, by the way, that added experience of Laidlay's play has forced me to the conclusion that a man *can* play golf in that style. Still, at the time I was left with a very poor opinion of the Scottish amateur.

CHAPTER II

My attempts at a first-class career may be said to have commenced in 1887. For the two previous years, between the ages of sixteen and eighteen, I hardly touched a club, chiefly for the reason that the opportunity was lacking; for when you leave your domicile for commerce at nine o'clock in the morning and, on the average, arrive back about seven o'clock at night, there is not much time for the royal and ancient game. The only exercise I then obtained was a little Saturday afternoon cricket.

However, in the spring of 1887 I joined the Royal Liverpool Golf Club, and as the championship was to take place at Hoylake, I arranged to take my holiday at the time it was to be held. I had a whole week's practice previous to the event, and during that week had two rounds with Johnnie Ball. I was told that he had not touched a club for some six weeks before he played those rounds, but it did not seem to make much difference to him. On both occasions he was round in a score comfortably under 80, and naturally I was beaten; but I was quite pleased with the trial, as the excellence of his play did not affect my game, and I stuck to him well. When the entry was published, I came to the conclusion that I had quite a good chance of doing some good, as the entries amounted to only 33, and in point of class it was far and away the poorest that has ever entered for the event.

Where were all the Scottish cracks? It is said that they stayed away, being under the impression that it was no use attempting to beat Johnnie Ball over his own course. Round number one I tackled in quite a light-hearted manner, having been told I was sure to beat my man, John Sharp of Dundee. In the end I won readily enough. I chiefly remember him for the enormous cigars he smoked all the way round. He did not seem to take championships very seriously. In round number two I was con-

fronted by the late Mr. John Ball, sen., and when
we arrived on the tee he remarked, "They all
say it is no use me coming out to play you,
but dang it all I am going to try!" And try
he did. I could not get away from him. Twice
I was one up, but he always dragged me back
again, and when once he took the lead comparatively close to home it was all over. I went
absolutely to pieces from nothing else than pure
funk. The only consolation I could eventually
derive was the fact that my conqueror very
nearly beat Horace Hutchinson in the penultimate round. The final of that championship
was witnessed by about fifty people only. There
is a photograph in the Royal Liverpool Club-
house depicting Horace Hutchinson putting at
the seventh hole. The crowd, if the gathering
is worthy of such a title, appear to be standing within a few feet of the players. What
a difference nowadays, with the thousands of
spectators, necessitating ropes and numberless
stewards!

Horace   Hutchinson   eventually   won   that
championship, but I have always thought that

he was lucky to do so, as at the beginning of the meeting he was playing very poorly; and although he improved as the week wore on, and played well in the final round, still Johnnie Ball was dreadfully unlucky in that he broke his pet wooden club going to the sixteenth hole, and recourse to a new club resulted in missed tee shots at both the seventeenth and eighteenth holes. I must confess that my first experience of a championship was not a happy one. I felt very subdued and chastened in spirit.

In 1888, although I practically played no golf, I had a try for the medal at the Spring Meeting of the club. I began the round at 8.30, the unearthly hour beloved by Jack Graham. My start was not an impressive one, as, with a strong following wind behind, my approach overran the green at the first hole—now the eighteenth—and I finished in the drain beyond the green. I chased my ball up and down that drain for some minutes, and finally holed out in thirteen. Thirteen is always an unlucky number, and I didn't win that medal.

In 1889, however, a change of occupation

gave me more opportunities of practising. At
the Spring Meeting of the Royal Liverpool Club
I met Laidlay for the first time. I had come
down in the afternoon of the day previous
to the meeting for a practice round. Laidlay
was in the club-house, and the late John Ball,
sen., introduced us. I eventually won the
match on the seventeenth green, but in doing
so I holed some terribly long putts. It was
not so much the winning of the match as a
casual remark I heard Laidlay make just afterwards that gave me the most pleasure. A friend
of his, on hearing of the result, remarked: "Well,
Johnnie, you are having a bad time." I was
within earshot and heard the reply: "That
man's a good player." It meant much from a
golfer of Laidlay's calibre.

Shortly after this I made my second appearance in the amateur event, and strangely
enough I was drawn against Laidlay straight
away. He beat me on the last green, a
result possibly justified on the play. Whilst
I was quite satisfied with the result in running
such a player to the last green, I have always

thought that I might even have done better had I played with more resolution at the times when I had a chance. At one period I had a lead of one, and the prospect of winning so frightened me that I went to pieces for the next three holes. I am afraid I began that round with the idea that if I gave mine enemy a good run I should have done well, and when the match had finished I felt I had done well. But that is not the spirit in which to approach a championship. You must go out to win whatever your chance may be on paper. Young Gordon Barry emphasised this fact at Prestwick.

Apart from my own game against Laidlay, I always remember this championship on account of the game between Johnnie Ball and Laidlay in the penultimate round. In losing the match at the twentieth hole, I have never seen a man have harder lines than Johnnie had. His second shot with a cleek seemed perfection— it was never off the pin; possibly a few of the spectators thought it might be in the small bunker beyond the hole, but I feel assured

that the majority thought that it was safe on
the green.   All doubts were set at rest, however,
when a prominent member of the Royal and
Ancient Club signalled " down." I have always
doubted whether his action was quite in accordance with golfing etiquette, as Laidlay had
yet to play, and it is occasionally an advantage
to know when your opponent is trapped.   Perhaps it made no difference to Laidlay's approach,
which was perfectly played, but the game of
golf is between the two players and their
caddies, and this some spectators do not seem
quite to realise.

In this year (1889) I came on a great deal
in my game, and when I finished up the year
I was handicapped within two strokes of Johnnie
Ball.

In 1890 the championship was played at
Hoylake.   I got through three rounds, and
then came across that great stumbling-block,
John Ball, jun.   This was one of the years in
which he treated all his opponents in somewhat summary fashion ; but I managed to do
better than the majority, as he only beat me

on the sixteenth green, and towards the middle of the round I certainly held the lead. But the old frightened, anxious spirit once again, as at St. Andrews, made itself evident. It was a year, however, in which the prowess of Johnnie Ball distinctly dominated the meeting, and never in the final of a championship has a more brilliant start been made than Johnnie made that year. I remember well the match had to be postponed owing to a thunderstorm. This seemed to suit him well, as he began putting like a demon. He would not be denied, and actually stood six up at the turn. Laidlay made a big fight coming home, but it was not a bit of good.

In this year I won my first big open tournament, and this was at North Berwick in the fall of the year. It was not a championship, and I went up with decided hopes of success. On the first night I arrived a very amusing incident happened in the smoking-room of the Marine Hotel. I was standing by the fireplace talking to Freddie Tait, and a prominent member of the Tantallon Club came in. He evidently did not recognise either of us, as on being asked who he thought was going to win, he promptly replied, "Well, they all say one of the two youngsters, Tait and Hilton; but I don't believe in them. I prefer the pluck of an old one." There was silence for a moment, and then a general titter. For a moment he looked surprised, but some one saved the situation by remarking, "Perhaps you would like to meet Tait and Hilton," and we were solemnly introduced. He was not put out a bit, as he immediately remarked, "Well, I am very glad to meet you; but, as I said before, I do not think either of you will win." He was wrong, however, as the second of the youngsters did win. In arriving at this end, and in the light of after events, he was possibly a little fortunate in not having to meet the other youngster. David Anderson, of Monifieth, kindly removed youngster number one from the pathway of youngster number two. This was one of the occasions on which Freddie Tait did have hard lines. The game stood all even and one to play, and Freddie hit one of his longest, with a bit of draw upon it. The ball careered along until it finished up in a sandy pathway, right against Hutchison's shop.   It was not a particularly nice lie, even if he could have played it right-handed ; but he could not possibly get at it this way, and eventually he had to send into the shop to borrow a left-handed niblick. Considering everything he made a wonderful recovery, but not sufficiently good enough to obtain the requisite half in four.

In connection with this tournament I witnessed one of the pluckiest and most extraordinary " get outs " I have ever seen in my life.   It was in a match between Arthur Molesworth and John Forrest—the latter, a local artisan, being strongly fancied on the short, tricky course that North Berwick then was.   There was more than glory to be gained in the winning of that match, as its possibilities raised a speculative spirit. Driving from the eighteenth tee, Forrest stood dormie one.   He hit quite a good tee shot, but Molesworth topped his into the road ; he ploughed the ball out, and played his third to the left of the green, about fifteen yards from the hole.   In the meantime his opponent had put his approach within about four yards of the hole, certainly not more. Molesworth was playing two more, and even if he holed his approach—as it certainly was more an approach than a putt—Forrest still had two more for the match. Oh, the time Molesworth took over that shot! Up and down he walked, time after time; in fact, so long was he that eventually one of a very partisan crowd made an audible remark, which was certainly not in strict accordance with the etiquette of the game, or in keeping with the solemnity of the occasion. Molesworth was not at all disconcerted; he simply turned round to the spectator and tersely remarked, "I suppose you think I am not going to hole this; you'll see," and hole it he did, using a long-shafted driving-cleek. Now came the other man's turn—four yards from the hole and two for the match, and that on a good green. He was using a wooden putter; I can remember it well. His approach putt was short, and also dragged across the hole to the left, the ball being left about three feet from the hole. The final effort was even worse, as it never looked like reaching its destination. The end came at the nineteenth hole, which Molesworth easily won. I was particularly interested in this finish as I had to meet the winner, and he supplied me with the hardest game I had in the tournament.

This success gave me confidence, and when I entered for the Amateur Championship in 1891, I had for the first time an idea that I had some slight chance of winning, the chief aid to this end being the avoidance of John Ball, jun., whose golfing virtues I knew far too well. In this respect the draw was very kind to me, as I was drawn far away from him, and what was more, nearly all the well-known players were in the half in which he was drawn. There were two men in my half of whom I was very much afraid; the first was F. A. Fairlie and the other David Leitch. The latter I had every reason to fear, as in previous practice he had very ably demonstrated to me how St. Andrews should be played. But fortune was on my side; Fairlie was ill and had to scratch, and Wharton Tod obligingly removed Leitch from the competition—a real surprise, as at that time David Leitch was just about the best amateur golfer over St. Andrews. I have always felt very thankful to Wharton Tod for that effort.

Eventually I reached the final, and had to meet my old enemy, Laidlay. As in 1889, I had the worst of the game. He took the lead at the third hole, where I missed a short putt for the half, upon which failure some of the crowd sympathetically clapped their hands. I once drew level, but was three down at the turn. Then came a change. I won the tenth and eleventh, and had all the best of the twelfth, as in two strokes I was just below the plateau, and Laidlay was some five or six yards from the hole in three. My third was quite a simple shot to play, as I had not to allow for anything but the rise of the hill. What did I do? I took my eye off the ball, hit the ground behind it, and never even reached the plateau, as the ball quietly rolled back almost to the same place from which I had attempted to play it. I eventually lost that hole, a hole which I looked like winning. It was a big turning-point in the game, as Laidlay was now two up, a lead he increased to three up with five to play.   By the time the seven-teenth had been holed out I had managed to get two of these holes back.   The last hole was against the wind.   We were both well short of the green in two.   He played his approach first, a very fair shot.   I considerably improved upon this, as my pitch ran quite close up to the feet of old Tom, who was standing at the hole.   I could not tell quite how close it was, and was agree-ably surprised when I came up to find that it was within two feet of the hole.   Laidlay missed his long putt, and I had that two-footer to halve the match.   For the first time during the game I felt really nervous.   It flashed through my mind, "What a fool you will be if you miss this!" but I managed to scramble it in, and then came hole number nineteen.   I have always considered that I was robbed of that hole — certainly legitimately robbed — as my opponent deserved the half he obtained on account of the beautiful run up he played, but at one time it looked any odds on my winning my first championship.   My tee shot was not of the best, as I got slightly under it.   Laidlay's

was some twenty yards farther. When I came
up to my ball I found that it was lying in a
freshly cut divot mark; in any case the carry
was a long one for me, but the lie made it all
the more difficult. Coming to the conclusion
that he was sure to get over in two, I decided
to have a go for it, and it came off. I nearly
hit the pin, and ran about five or six yards
past the hole. Laidlay hesitated for a moment,
and then took his cleek, with which he played
a really wicked shot, as he hooked it right
round. It cleared the burn, chiefly on account
of the fact that the burn bends in towards the
player at that point. Even although he was
over, however, I felt quite in clover, for he had
one of the most difficult shots in the world to
play, as he could not possibly pitch the shot,
and in running the stroke he had of necessity
to just trickle it over the hill. The slightest
extra pace would have put him yards past the
pin, as the hole was placed on the left-hand
corner of the green. That shot came off. It
was beautifully played, and deserved to finish
where it did, that is, within three feet of the

hole, with the result that a half in four was called. The next hole saw the end. I simply threw it away, as I had all the best of the tee shot, and could have reached home with my second; but, thinking that a very indifferent second of my opponent's was bunkered on the left—as it happened it was not—I played far too safely on the right; I paid the penalty by getting a lie in a divot mark on an old teeing ground, and from there fooled about until I had taken six to hole out. Still, a silver medal was an improvement on previous performances, and I could see the possibility of a gold one in the future. How long I had to wait for it is recorded in history.

This year I made my bow in the open championship and did fairly well, as I finished second amateur, Mure Fergusson being first, and in the whole list tied with Willie Auchterlonie, then playing as an amateur, for seventh place. Up to that time I had seen little either of professionals or professional golf. The latter, I knew, could not be very much better than that of the best amateur description, as Johnnie Ball had somewhat easily won the Open Championship at Prestwick in the previous year. As regards the professionals themselves, I knew literally nothing outside our home professionals at Hoylake. I had always heard, however, that they were chiefly persons who were invariably willing to back themselves to beat anything walking or crawling, and my first experience of them tended to confirm this reputation.

I was standing by the last green when an individual came up to me, and, without a word of preface, suggested that he was willing to do something. I could not grasp his broad Doric, and begged his pardon for not being able to do so. On a repetition of what I had come to the conclusion must be a challenge of some description, I found out that he wished to back his score against mine on the morrow. Never having seen the man before, I was a little taken aback, not to say annoyed, and replied, "I have not the faintest idea who you are, and if I had I should certainly not bet with you." I afterwards found out that he was a player whose name was not unknown in connection with championship honours in the past, and I may remark he would have just annexed my sovereign. This championship was quite an excellent experience, which probably stood me in good stead in the following year.

1892 was my first big year. My past championship experiences had been of great service to me. I had by degrees realised the various essentials which a man must possess if he wishes to win championships. First, it was essential that the player should go out to win. The feeling that if you got through a round or two and then ran a big man very close, may be an eminently satisfactory attitude of mind for a youngster, but is of no use for winning championships. Whatever your chance might be, you had to go for the gloves, was an impression left on my mind, and these impressions certainly stood me in good stead at Sandwich in the amateur event. I had quite a favourable position in the draw, and took every advantage of it by reaching the penultimate round, when I had to meet my conqueror of 1889 and 1891, John Laidlay. I had been playing better than ever I had done in my life, and I felt there was a good prospect of reversing the old order of affairs. My confidence was not misplaced, as I took the lead early in the round, and, never looking back, won on the fourteenth green.

Having disposed of one crack, I now had to meet another, viz., John Ball, jun. Now Johnnie had not been playing his usual accurate game at that meeting. His task had been a hard one, as he had been given a lot of difficult men to beat. In the very first round it appeared a moral certainty that his chance of championship honours had gone for the year, as he was four down at the tenth hole, and, what was worse, had missed his second to the eleventh. But his opponent, Andy Stuart, then made a most fatal blunder, topping his second into the bunker on the ridge guarding the green, and losing a hole which he certainly should have halved, if not won. The incident seemed to have a demoralising effect on his play, as he could do no good afterwards and was eventually beaten.

Again, against Leslie Balfour and Horace

Hutchinson, Johnnie only just got home by holing very missable putts on the last green, and that after being four up on each of them at one time. But " all's well that ends well," and he reached the final, where I had to meet him. It was not a great game as regards play, but there was never much in it, and at the twelfth hole we stood all square. Then came one of those little turns of fortune which tend to decide a match. At the thirteenth hole he ran down quite a longish putt for a four, and at the same time for the hole.

To the fourteenth I had the best of the wooden club play, my second being quite close to the bunker guarding the green, whilst his was some way short, and as the approach was down wind and the green keen, I held a distinct advantage. His approach was not a good one; it was far too merry and looked like finishing in the rushes beyond the green, but it struck the guiding post on the far edge of the green and bounced back. My third finished some seven or eight yards past the pin. His run up he played beautifully, and nearly holed it, the ball finishing about a foot

past the hole. Now my approach putt had to
be played on a slippery green with a ball just
beyond the hole. The rules of golf decree that
if your opponent's ball is in the way and the
distance between the balls is more than six inches,
you have to play your ball as it lies. This fact
crossed my mind and I played this approach
putt very gingerly, with the result that I was
five feet short and then missed the subsequent
putt. I was now two down and my chances
were quickly vanishing away. The climax came
at the fifteenth. With our approaches we were
both on the line to the left of the hole, and
were left with most difficult approach putts. I
had to play first and was far too strong. He
played and was also too strong ; but the ball met
the hole, took a leap in the air and fell in, thus
concluding a somewhat cruel sequence. The end
came on the seventeenth green. I always consider that this was the only final I ever played
in which fortune was a little unkind to me,
and I have played in five.

After this came my success at Muirfield. The
circumstances under which I happened to go to

Muirfield were somewhat peculiar and interesting. A few weeks before the event I had no intention of going, chiefly for the reason that I did not think it was worth the financial outlay; but a week or so before the meeting I received an invitation from a friend to come and stay with him during the meeting. I have always been thankful to him ever since for that invitation; had it not come I should certainly not have been present. Still, invitation thrown in, I could not make up my mind, chiefly for the reason that I knew the parental wishes were against such a proceeding, and the parental wishes in those days also coincided with those of the employer. Eventually I summoned up courage to suggest that I should like to go—this being about four o'clock on the Monday afternoon, and the championship began on Wednesday. The suggestion was not received with acclamation or loud cheers, but finally the words came forth, " Well, go if you *want* to go; but I cannot see much use in your going." As I *wanted* badly, I wasted no time, and was off by the midnight train.

Just one day for practice, and I made full use of it, as I played three rounds, a rather austere training for a championship on top of an all-night journey. I remember the first round I managed to beat the record of the course, and this so impressed my opponent, Garden Smith, that he promptly foraged round to find some one who would lay odds against me, and was eventually rewarded with the remunerative odds of four to one. Not feeling quite safe, he also backed Willie Park at the same odds; then when I told him I thought Johnnie Ball would win, four to one was also taken about Johnnie, and he found himself in the happy financial position of having laid the odds of six to four on three players against the field. As it happened, the wager came off all right, and he was quite justified when he afterwards remarked that he who laughs last laughs best.

My first round in the championship was quite fair, viz., 78—four strokes behind the leader, Horace Hutchinson. The commencement of my second round was terrible. The first six holes were holed out in 29, only one under fives; but worse was to follow, as I found my tee shot lying up against a thistle, of which there were a goodly number at Muirfield in those days. The carry on to the green was over the bunker which at present guards the short hole coming in, but in 1892 it was an infinitely worse hazard than it is to-day. I foolishly decided to go for it, and paid the penalty, as I got up to my neck in the sand, and taking three to get out, eventually holed out in seven. Now I happened to have two side wagers on my score, and this fact probably saved me from going to pieces, as I played to save them, and by the aid of a good finish, got round in 81, eight strokes behind the leader, once again Horace Hutchinson. On day number two, however, there was a different tale to tell. I could hardly do any wrong. I began by nearly holing out the first hole in one. The late Mr. Edward Blyth, who was at the hole, told me that he could not understand how the ball did not stay in the hole. After that came a succession of fours, until the eighth hole was reached—that is, the present long fifth hole ; there I met with a temporary check, as from the tee I found a pot bunker, which has since been filled up, and a six was recorded ; but a mashie shot laid stone dead at the ninth enabled me to get out in 35, just ten strokes better than my total of the previous round.   Homeward I threw little away, and finished in 72, a score which at a bound threw me into second place, three strokes behind Johnnie Ball.

Now my last round was a lucky one.   I commenced most unpromisingly with a four and a six ; then came the first piece of fortune, as, after pushing my second out at the third, I actually holed my little pitch of about twenty yards ; to any one who knows that third green at Muirfield, the value of this shot can readily be understood.   It is certainly the most tricky putting-green on the course, and, what was more, that shot gave me heart of grace.   At hole number six another of these pleasing accidents occurred, but this time the distance was not so long, and certainly it was a much easier shot.   These two unexpected threes were mainly instrumental in my getting out in 38, as on the whole my golf had not been the soundest of the sound. Just then I heard a spectator remark, " He has a 76 to win," thus leaving me 38 for the homeward journey, which was much shorter than the outward half. I commenced the task well, as the first three holes, the present seventh, eighth, and ninth, were all fours, and I made my position more secure by laying a mashie shot stone dead at the next. A four and a three followed, and I began to think I must have a little bit in hand—how much I didn't dare to think. I had a clear green, and was travelling at a terrible pace, fairly running my poor partner, Jacky Ferguson, off his legs, Then we had to wait on the tee, and I heard a spectator say, " Oh, he can't lose unless he has a fit and falls down dead ; he has eighteen for the last three to win." It might be thought that this remark would instil confidence into my soul, but on the other hand it made me anxious, and I played the sixteenth hole terribly safe, pitching my approach right over the green, and I was eventually hard pushed to get down in five. At the next, a shortish hole, played over the bunker guarding the present twelfth hole, I heaved a sigh of relief when they signalled all clear, as I had got under the ball a little. A three was registered there, which left me with an eight for the last to win. There was only about one way I could lose, and that was by topping my tee shot into the bunker at my feet; I avoided that mistake, and, taking no risks, carefully holed out in six.

Now when I look back at that round I cannot but realise that fortune was very much on my side. Firstly, I holed two mashie pitches. General report had it afterwards that I was holing iron shots all over the green. This was not true, as the aggregate length of the two shots was probably not more than forty yards, and on many greens it would not have been necessary to use an iron at all, as a putter would have sufficed. But in 1892 Muirfield was quite a new green, and the putting-greens were very small indeed, and the grass just off the green was invariably very rough. Still, considering the conditions and the state of the game, these two shots were very useful. Then again, in that round I must have holed at least six or seven very missable putts, some of them as long as nine or ten feet, and this holing out does tell in the scoring game.

I have always had an idea that the fact that I had enjoyed about three months' practice over the Formby course was of great assistance to me in this Muirfield championship. The greens there were somewhat similar in size to those at Muirfield, and in consequence there was a good deal of the pitching from the rough at the edge of green which was such a feature of the play at Muirfield in 1892.

To conclude, I may say that when I went up North I had no designs upon the championship. My ambition leaned towards the amateur event. To me it seemed silly to win the open event before the amateur, and after the event I could not realise that I had secured the bigger prize before the lesser.

CHAPTER III

In 1893 I commenced my golfing career as a man with a reputation—a reputation begotten of my success in the Open Championship. I must candidly acknowledge that the burden did not sit heavily on my shoulders, since in many respects I quite agreed with the numerous critics who averred that I was lucky to win at Muirfield, and moreover that I should never have won had the competition been played over a links which, as a test of the game, might be considered worthy of the occasion. With both these propositions I in the main agree, as in my own mind I had no other idea but that on the second day I was distinctly the favourite of fortune, and the short length and the conformation of the links were quite suited to my style of play. I have therefore always felt very grateful to the Honourable Company of Edinburgh Golfers for robbing

Musselburgh of its ancient birthright and transferring the championship to Muirfield, and have ever since maintained that they were quite right in so doing.   As regards the justice of the act I am afraid I had not a sufficient knowledge of the subject to form an opinion.

My first effort to uphold my reputation as a champion golfer was not at all successful.   The event was the Amateur Championship at Prestwick and it was an occasion which provided Freddie Tait with his maiden effort at my expense. The draw decreed that we should meet in the first round.   I believe I was a decided favourite for the heat, and I know of one or two people who laid considerable odds upon me.   They eventually had to pay, however, as I was beaten on the sixteenth green, simply for the reason that I missed literally every holeable putt.   The hole seemed very small that day.   I did not think much of this defeat at the time, but had I been able to look into the future I should probably have viewed it in a very different light.

This championship at Prestwick was one of the most peculiar I have ever witnessed.   Eventually the young St. Andrews student, Peter Anderson, proved the winner; but apart from any question as to whether on his play he deserved his success, there can be little doubt that fate was kind to him. Firstly, in order to reach the semi-final round he had no men of great note to meet; when he reached that semi-final round he was confronted by a player who in the previous heats had been playing very fine golf— that player was Mure Fergusson—but who, when he came to play on the last day, was suffering from a severe attack of gout, which must have had a very serious effect upon his play. He could not put any pressure on his foot without feeling great pain, and in the case of a free swinger, as he undoubtedly is, this must have seriously affected his long game. In the final round Peter Anderson had to meet Laidlay, and the odds appeared considerably in favour of the latter, who about that time was quite at his best, as he proved later in the year in the Open Championship. But in this final his game was far below what it had been, and eventually he was beaten on the last green.

I always remember one shot he played in that match, which had a very considerable effect on the result. Going to the third hole, Anderson, who had half missed his tee shot, had been obliged to play his second well to the left, so as to take the narrow angle of the "Cardinal" bunker. Laidlay had hit a magnificent tee shot just short of the "Cardinal," and could have almost got home with another good one. What did he do? he absolutely hit the ball hard on the top, and put it into the bunker right under his feet! In consequence he lost a hole which he had an excellent chance of winning. It was a disastrous mistake, particularly as he had won the first two holes, and at the time it looked as if he would run away with the game. I cannot help thinking that that one frightful error had an effect on his after play, as he certainly did not thereafter play up to his previous form.

It was a peculiar and sensational championship, as Peter Anderson won and deserved to win on account of his pluck alone, and big names did not frighten him in the least. Still the

other semi-finalists—Freddie Tait, Laidlay, and
Mure Fergusson—had much severer work to accomplish, and on their play any one of them
deserved to win. I have always thought that
the last-mentioned of this trio would have about
won that championship had not that attack of
gout found him out.

Mure Fergusson has not been a fortunate man
in championships. Twice has he been in the
final, and on one of these occasions, viz., at
Hoylake in 1898, he had the most cruel luck.
But this is a tale of after years and must wait.
In 1893 at Prestwick he was undoubtedly playing well, and although it may have been that had
he met Laidlay, the latter would have played
better than he did against Peter Anderson,
still Mure Fergusson had a very big chance
that year.

It so happened that the Open Championship,
as well as the amateur event, took place at
Prestwick in 1893. I always remember a headline which appeared in a Glasgow evening paper
on the first day of the tournament. It read as
follows: " Hilton not to be champion again."

The headline was more than justified, for my very first round ended in terrible disaster. I was out in 37 ; no man could claim a lower total, and I commenced the homeward journey with two fives. Then a gentle little ten crept in, most of the strokes being expended in close vicinity to the wall.

What happened was this. A slightly fluffed approach, played from the right, landed right on the top of the wall, bounded up in the air, and fell on the wrong side of the hazard. For some time the ball could not be seen, but eventually it was found firmly wedged in between the wall and a bunch of star grass. The first attempt to dislodge it was very carefully thought out, as not being able to see the ball unless I viewed it from the perpendicular, I had to take a good view and then diagnose its position. My first diagnosis was wrong, or perhaps my aim was at fault. Attempt number two had an equally futile result; then, without changing my stance, I tried what brute force would do. I hit hard at the spot at which I thought " she " was resting, and out " she " came; brute force and temper had prevailed where care and equanimity had failed. It is not always thus in the game of golf.

Eventually a ten was recorded, a very serious handicap even in days when one could afford to make an occasional serious mistake. Now-a-days a really serious mistake literally puts one out of court. The next six holes I played in a state of semi-demoralisation. Sixes crept in with alarming frequency, and I finished in 88, no less than 51 of these strokes being expended upon these homeward nine holes. The result was the aforesaid press notice, " Hilton not to be champion again "—a notice quite justified by the result, as, notwithstanding three very good rounds, I finished ten strokes behind the winner —ten strokes all lost in that one half round; in fact, all lost in seven holes.

That year the championship was won by Willie Auchterlonie, probably one of the biggest surprises in the history of the game, as, except on his native St. Andrews, he was quite an unknown quantity. There must have been some one, however, who appreciated his talent, as a professional bookmaker tried his luck at making a book on the event, and some one had the temerity to back Auchterlonie at fifty to one. The "bookie" afterwards remarked, "There are some people who seem to know something about this game; I've finished with it."

This championship of 1893 will always remain memorable on account of the fact that it was the occasion of the *début* of both Harry Vardon and Taylor. At the time little was known about Vardon, but Taylor had come up North with the reputation of being a most promising recruit to professional golf, and in the play previous to the actual championship he more than justified this reputation. He took all the cracks on in turn, and flattened them out. The Scottish contingent could not make it out; there was still greater consternation when, in the very first round, he handed in a card of 75, a score quite unthought of, and tongues began to wag rapidly about the new prodigy. The occasion, however, proved too much for the then novice, and from a first attempt of 75 he fell in his second to 86, and eventually finished in tenth position. It was, however, an excellent experience for him, which he turned to good account next year at Sandwich.

Harry Vardon in the meanwhile was pursuing the even tenor of his way quite unnoticed. Yet he holed the first five holes in a very low total —something like 18—and then went to pieces; but it was at this meeting that one or two of us realised the possibilities in his game, and I always thought from that time that he had the makings of a very great player.

Auchterlonie won that championship, but I have always held the opinion that there was another player in the field who might readily have gained the honour had he taken advantage of his opportunities, and that was Mr. Laidlay. He finished second, two strokes behind the winner, but time after time he threw his chances away by playing too much for safety. I happened to be playing with him on the second day, so that I saw the whole of his two rounds, and I have no hesitation in saying that had he on occasions exhibited a little more enterprise he might readily have added the title of open champion to his previous honours. But directly he seemed to have a winning chance he threw it away by playing too safely. From the confident and accurate way he was playing there certainly seemed no necessity for safety play.

One of the unlucky ones in that championship was the late Hugh Kirkaldy. He was well to the front on the first day, and was doing exceptionally well in the third round; in fact, going to the fifteenth hole he was leading the whole field. To this hole his tee shot was on the plateau, short of the pot bunker. His second, played with a wooden club, the wind being dead against him, was boldly played, but he got a slight pull on the ball, or perhaps it would be more correct to say, that he held a little too much into the wind. The ball hovered in the air, apparently doubtful whether to come down straight into the bunker or swerve on to the green, but eventually it decided to be perverse, and down it came into the bunker. And what a lie! Men had been there before, and the hoof marks were deep and many. Poor Hugh found one, with the result that the hole cost him eight strokes.   Now Auchterlonie in the same round played this fifteenth in almost identical fashion; but his second shot just cleared the hazard, and rolling down the hill, eventually finished sufficiently near for him to hole out in three, and it may be mentioned that at the time he was doing none too well.

The year 1894 was not a particularly fortunate one for me.   I commenced my championship career by once again suffering defeat at the hands of Freddie Tait, and this on my home green at Hoylake.   It was a game rather devoid of interest—at least, from the sensational point of view.   I well remember winning the first two holes, and feeling somewhat confident.   Walking to the third tee, a perfervid supporter of Hoylake golf walked up to me, and, slapping me on the back, remarked, "That's right, old man ; rub it into him."   No doubt he meant well, but an important golf match is not the time to slap a man on the back.   Golf is not wrestling, or even football, where such behaviour may be perhaps tolerated.   Two up in two holes is what may be termed a useful dividend to collect, but it quickly dwindled away, and eventually I found myself one down with two to play. Going to the seventeenth hole — now the sixteenth, or " Dun " hole — I put my approach within a few feet of the hole, and felt quite happy about it ; but Freddie improved upon this, and put his approach inside mine. As it happened, we both missed silly little putts, his miss taking place after mine and just saving my skin. The only incident at the last hole was the fact that he had a putt of about fifteen inches to win the match, and very nearly missed it, the ball going right round the rim and then resting on the lip before it fell back into the hole. In the following round Freddie failed rather badly against Mure Fergusson, being beaten by four up and three to play, and that after holding a lead on the outward journey.

The final in this championship between John Ball, jun., and Mure Fergusson was a memorable one. The former won the first four holes, and all seemed over ; but he could get no " forrarder," and was surely and slowly pegged back. Holes kept disappearing with varying frequency until the whole four had vanished, with but two to play. There was naturally a good deal of excitement, and Scotland's representatives were wildly exuberant in their anticipations; and I remember one well-known Scottish golfer shouting out, " Johnnie Ball's beaten ; he's funking." I didn't see him after the event, but it is more than probable that when he had seen the seventeenth hole played he had altered his key. There the gentleman who was presumed to be funking brought off a shot which will live in the memory of all who saw it. It was one of those strokes which will be handed down to history. Mure Fergusson had a fair drive ; Johnnie Ball had a really good one, right down on to the old race-course. The former played very short with his second. Johnnie hesitated a moment, and then went for the green. He hit his ball as true as steel, and the ball in its flight hardly ever left the pin, and finished up just beyond the hole. It was a really *big* shot played at a trying moment, and just when it was wanted. He won that hole, and a half at the last hole sufficed.

The Open Championship that year was played at Sandwich, and it was a championship in which the superiority of the professional over his amateur brother was marked in a very decided, not to say unpleasant, manner—unpleasant at least to those who held a more or less decided opinion that the unpaid golfer was nearly, if not quite, as good as the paid. And they certainly had some justification in this belief, as in the previous four years twice had an amateur been successful, and Mr. Laidlay had run up to Auchterlonie in the previous year. In fact, considering the disparity in the number of the players taking part in the event, the leading amateurs had quite held their own with the professionals. There was a rude awakening at Sandwich in 1894, as there were nearly twenty strokes between the winner (Taylor) and Lieutenant Tait, the first of the amateurs. It was certainly Freddie Tait who saved the reputations of the amateurs at that meeting. In the amateur and professional tournament which took place after the championship he reached the penultimate round, and only succumbed to Douglas

Rolland on the twentieth green in a game about which there are mixed opinions; but more of this anon.

To revert to the personal. My own participation in the event proper ended at the thirteenth hole in the second round, where I found a bunker in front of the green, in which were stones and rocks of various sizes; and I eventually decided to play the rest of the round without troubling the marker. Not that this individual visitation at all affected the destination of the championship; I had dissipated my chance in other hazards long before. There was a very plausible excuse, however, and that was that, just seventeen days before the championship, I was practising with a new club which Douglas M'Ewan, then stationed at Musselburgh, had in the fulness of his heart made and presented to me. The club was not fashioned in the handle to suit my grip, with the result that, when I was playing the seventh hole at Formby, my right hand in the downward swing lost command of the club, leaving all the weight on the left hand. The consequence was that I hit the ground hard, and in doing so I tore the main sinew leading to the first finger and thumb clean away from the sheathing which binds the sinews together in the wrist. I did not think much of the incident at the moment; but thought more of it when I came to play my next stroke, as in the upward swing I had to let the club go out of my hands, the pain was so great. I went straight back to the club-house, and there met a doctor, who suggested the usual simple remedies of water and bandages, and then told me to try the wrist again in a few days. I did try it, and the result was disastrous, as after trying three gentle shots, I had a go with it at the fourth, and the pain was sufficient to suggest that there was something seriously wrong. It seemed to me as if some one had unkindly struck me across the wrist with a heavy stick. I wandered back to the club-house and once again interviewed my medical man, who at once advised me to consult Dr. Robert Jones, the well-known Liverpool specialist; Dr. Jones took about ten seconds to locate the injury, and promptly re-

E

marked, "You must not play for two or three months." The Open Championship was close at hand, and my keenness overcoming my discretion, I answered, "I must play at Sandwich the week after next." "Well," said the doctor, "if you do, it will probably always affect you." I took my own line of action, and underwent drastic treatment for the next ten days, with repeated "firing" and continuous wearing of splints, and I arrived at Sandwich without having used my left wrist for ten days.

Before the championship I played ten holes, but played them in a very gingerly fashion, and as previously recorded, I took the opportunity in the championship of picking up my ball at the hole number thirteen in the second round, reserving myself for the St. George's Vase, which was played immediately after the big event. I won the Vase, and I always consider that it was the finest performance I ever accomplished in my life. In the first place, I had to play with Freddie Tait; not that I wanted to at all, as even in those early days he had an effect upon my play, but I could not get out of it. Not being sure whether I could play or not, I had not arranged for a partner. I asked the Secretary, the late Mr. William Rutherford, whether he could find me one. Presently he came and said, " I have found you a partner—Freddie Tait." I thanked him as graciously as I could, but candidly I would rather have played with some one a little less terrible. It must have been a funny game to the spectator, as from every tee he literally lost me. I had to play with a very short club, and moreover a very short swing, my main object being to avoid any position which would necessitate a forcing stroke. In this I was very successful, as I circumvented the bunkers in the most approved fashion, and I did have a day out with my mashie. Time after time I laid my pitches within holing distances, with the result that at the end of the first round I held a lead of three strokes from my partner, and also from the rest of the field. Round number two was an even more crucial one, as my wrist was palpably beginning to tire; still, on the easy outward journey I once more avoided trouble, and succeeded in gaining another stroke on my opponent. But the trying homeward journey had now to be faced. At the tenth hole the lie from my tee shot presented me with a serious problem as regards distance. I could easily get over the bunker, but I was lying down hill in a divot mark—just the lie I did not want. Perhaps I should have played short, but I had a heave at it, and finished in the bunker, with the result that I dropped two of my lead of four strokes. I held my own at the next hole, but another stroke departed at the twelfth and another at the thirteenth, both of which holes had to be played more or less against the wind. The fourteenth hole at Sandwich is not a hole built for a lame duck, and much depended upon it. My tee shot was my usual short one; Tait's was, as usual, thirty or forty yards further. With my second I just managed to crawl over the water, the shot being a low hooked one, which eventually finished in the rough on the right hand side of the course. Freddie could have almost pitched his ball over with a mashie, but the stance an awkward one, the ball standing right away above him. He first of all addressed it with an iron club, then changed his mind and took a

wooden one and this ended in disaster, as he hit
it all along the ground into the water.   He had
to drop and play four.   This fourth was a beauty,
but the distance was too far, and he landed right
under the face of the bunker guarding the green.
To cut a long story short he holed out in seven,
and I scrambled a five, giving me a lead of two
strokes.   The next hole he was on the green in
two, and holed out perfectly in four.   I had to
rest content with a five.   At the sixteenth I obtained a hard half in four, but still I did not feel
at all safe with my simple lead of one stroke and
two holes to play.   The usual thing happened
from the next tee.   I was again miles behind,
but still I could reach the green, and that was
something; and I did reach it, with a stroke
which could not be far from the pin.   Mine enemy
obliged by hitting his approach off the socket,
and the lead was in consequence increased to two.
The same thing happened at the eighteenth.   I
put my second near the hole, and again a socketer
came in response, and eventually I won by three
strokes.   It was the only time I ever played
against Freddie Tait in which he may be said

to have in any way cracked, and he certainly did crack when playing those last two holes. A reader may here remark, "What about the rest of the field?" Well, to be candid, we both knew some way from home that we were literally the only two in it. One or two kindly spectators had not forgotten to tell us so. I may be excused in quoting this species of duel, as it was just about the only time in my life I ever could claim an advantage over Master Freddie, and the debit balance is certainly a heavy one.

To return to the championship proper, it ended in a signal triumph for Taylor, and he thoroughly justified the big opinions formed of him on his first appearance at Prestwick. I always remember the remark of a prominent St. George's member, who had followed Taylor assiduously. At the end of the third round I asked him whether Taylor was playing really well. He replied, "I don't know what you would call playing well, but as far as I can see he has only one hazard to fear from the tees, and that is the guide flags. I have never seen anything like it," and from all testimony which can be brought to bear on his performance he certainly must have been driving with wonderful accuracy. Towards the finish of his last round he naturally became a little anxious, and I can well remember him playing the fourteenth hole—the hole above all others at Sandwich which a player in a stroke competition likes to see behind him. It was played against the wind, and the sun was low and facing him. His tee shot was right down the middle; his second was not of the best, being low and slightly hooked, and it cleared the bank at the back of the water by a very narrow margin. His third, a wooden club shot, had to be played right in the face of the sun—a very trying stroke. He hit the ball well, but apparently with a suspicion of slice on it, as it went away to the right, and in the bright facing light it was difficult to say where it would finish. Taylor very apparently lost sight of it, and either knowing that he must have cut the shot, or else, judging by the anxious look on the faces of the spectators, felt that there was a doubt as to its safety. A shout that the ball was safe appeared to relieve him immensely, and after that it was plain sailing for him. He had passed the dreaded fourteenth.

This year, 1894, was one of the years in which Andrew Kirkaldy appeared likely at last to win a championship. At the end of the third round he was three strokes behind Taylor, who was leading. In the fourth round Andrew was out in 36—exceptionally fine golf at that time. I always remember the occasion, as I had backed Andrew to win outright at the odds of ten to one. At the turn a St. Andrews man came up to me and excitedly remarked, "Andrew is going to win." I acquiesced in the opinion, and seeing an opportunity of beneficial hedging, offered to lay him even money. He was at first a little suspicious, possibly thinking that I knew something, but on being told the circumstances of the original bet he quickly accepted the odds. Judging by the subsequent play I might be accorded the gift of second sight, as from that time forth Andrew played rubbish, finally finishing up by hitting his approach to the last hole right on the socket of his iron, the ball pitching on the reporter's tent, which was supposed to lie quite out of harm's way. Those last nine holes cost him no less than 48 strokes, and from what I saw of his play he deserved most of them.

After that championship the St. George's Club promoted an amateur and professional tournament; it was hoped that this would become an annual fixture, but the Royal and Ancient Club in the following year would have none of it. Personally I think it was a pity that it was not continued, as the amateur player has but few chances of meeting the professional in serious combat, and such opportunities would to my mind be of great benefit to amateur golf.

It was a most interesting event, and served to emphasise two facts — first, the superiority of the professional over the amateur, and second, the pluck and match-playing abilities of Lieutenant Frederick Guthrie Tait. There were eight amateurs selected and eight professionals, and in each case an amateur was drawn against a professional. Round number one saw six out of the eight amateurs bow the knee, the successful ones being Mr. John Ball, who just got home against Willie Park, and Lieutenant Tait, who somewhat easily beat Archie Simpson. I well remember Archie being somewhat disconsolate about his defeat, as some of the professionals *not* selected in the chosen eight had openly expressed their doubt as to his right to inclusion. In round number two Mr. Ball went down before Taylor, but Lieutenant Tait easily held his own against Willie Fernie, and then had to meet Douglas Rolland. What a game it was! Rolland won on the twentieth green, and on the run of the play deserved to win. He undoubtedly had the best of the long game, and consistently out-drove his opponent, who was not at his best from the tee; but in short approaching and putting there was only one in it, and that was not the professional. Indeed, it is more than probable that the fact that Rolland laid Freddie a stymie on the seventeenth green saved the former the match. In the final Rolland beat

Taylor, as he generally did about that time. Personally I have always looked upon that tournament as one of the most interesting in the history of the game, and it seems a pity that it has never been repeated.

CHAPTER IV

THE year 1895 is one which I cannot look back upon with any degree of satisfaction. In truth, in the big events I was an obsolete vessel. The injury to my wrist proved a severe handicap, as it was quite impossible for me to follow any continued course of practice; directly I did there were the most evident signs that the injury was still there, with the result that before any competition which required a more than average degree of continuous play, I had to refrain from playing. Before the Amateur Championship at St. Andrews I never touched a club for fully a week previous to the commencement of the tournament, and one usually loses that delicate touch of the instrument which is so essential even in an athletic game such as the game of golf.

My career in that championship at St. Andrews

was short, without being altogether inglorious, as I managed to get through one round, the enemy being a very worthy opponent in the person of my old friend, Charles Edward Dick. In round number two William Greig barred the way, and I had to cry enough at the sixteenth hole. I had no complaint to make about the match; it was simply that I was outplayed. It was not Greig's putting, for which he is famous, that did for me: it was the general average excellence of his game. It was rather a peculiar coincidence in the draw that there were three representatives of the Royal Liverpool Club very close together, and omitting John Ball, jun., these three members — Hutchings, Dick, and the writer—had probably the best chance of bringing the trophy to Hoylake. I well remember suggesting in the *Sporting Chronicle* that the proximity of these three in the draw was somewhat of a hardship to the cause of Hoylake golf. It was one of those usual growls about the iniquity of the draw. As it so happened, none of these three survived, as Greig defeated Charles Hutchings, and as mentioned before he also accounted for the last survivor in the following round. Perhaps they might have done better had they been separated, but the luck of the draw is all in the game, and William Greig cleared out a goodly portion of the Hoylake fleet.

The flagship of the fleet however, John Ball, jun., was still afloat, and for once in a way it may be said that he threw a championship away, as few who witnessed the final round when he played against Leslie Balfour-Melville will forget. To hark back to the earlier stages of the event, it must first be said that Freddie Tait was a very decided favourite; this favouritism was probably justified on form, but there can be little doubt that at St. Andrews in 1895 the Scottish portion of the spectators were quite Tait mad. Freddie had then risen to the position of a popular hero, and the majority would not listen to the possibility of defeat, this opinion being probably strengthened by the " wish being father to the thought." Well, everything went as merry as a marriage bell for the favourite. He reached the penultimate round without being severely stretched. Then there was a very serious stumbling-block to overcome — John Ball, jun., to wit. There have been very few matches in connection with the championship which have evoked greater interest. There was a delightful international flavour about the meeting of these two; they represented the respective hopes of Scotland and England, and moreover there was more than a little wagering on the result. The Scotsmen not only pinned their faith to Freddie Tait on account of his golfing ability; they argued to themselves that in the first place he was playing over his home green, to which he had always evinced a strong partiality, whilst in the second his enemy had never done well over the classic green, nor shown any strong liking for its peculiarities; and these little facts seemed to turn the balance in favour of the local man. Well, Freddie did not win, and moreover did not win a single hole. The fact that he had missed what appeared to be a very simple putt on the very first green seemed to have a demoralising effect on his play and, although it is always easy to be wise after the event, there certainly was a very decided impression amongst the onlookers that after the first few holes had been played he looked a beaten man. It was a crushing blow, and none felt it more keenly than the vanquished man himself. For a short time after the event he was just about the sickest man in Europe. I can sympathise with him—I have been through it myself.

Naturally a very large proportion of the spectators followed this Ball-Tait encounter, which ended in such a tame fashion. They would perhaps have been better employed in having a peep at semi-final number two, between Laurence Auchterlonie and Leslie Balfour. At that time Auchterlonie was undoubtedly playing a very fine game, and was strongly fancied by the townspeople; moreover that excellent judge of the game, Mr. H. S. C. Everard, had a strong predilection for his chance, and told me before the meeting began that he was sure to go very close. Had he taken advantage of his chance at the sixteenth hole he would certainly have reached the final. Auchterlonie was on the green in two, and withal quite close to the hole—two magnificent shots against the wind. His opponent was all over the course, but finally ran down a long putt for five. Auchterlonie still had two for the hole, but his nerve apparently deserted him, as he putted wide with his approach putt, and then missed a very short one. Notwithstanding this disaster however, he still stood dormie one; but the champion, who was to be, saved himself at the eighteenth by putting his second—a full wooden club shot—within a few inches of the hole, and the end came at the burn, where Auchterlonie's hopes of the championship found a watery grave—the result of stroke number two.

The final was viewed in the light of a good thing for Hoylake, and the Hoylake gamblers did not hesitate to lay substantial odds on their man, a piece of temerity which they eventually had occasion to rue. At the third hole the odds appeared quite justified, as Balfour-Melville stood three holes in arrear; but he never gave up heart, and gradually these holes came back. Then the

F

luck went all against the Hoylake man, one piece of ill fortune at the thirteenth hole being particularly exasperating; from a good drive the ball lodged in a little grassy pot, hard against a shallow face, and on Johnnie attempting to play it, it struck the face, bounced back, and hit the club—result, a lost hole. Finally, in place of Balfour-Melville being three down, he stood in the comfortable position of dormie two.

Now came another change, as Johnnie Ball won the last two holes. The burn once again came into evidence at this nineteenth hole. Both were short with their seconds. Balfour-Melville pitched over safely, but there was a smothered groan when it was seen that Johnnie Ball had gone right under his ball. To spectators some distance off it was a doubtful question as to whether it would clear the water or not, but quickly came the fatal splash, and the championship was as good as over. In a sense, this fatal pitch at the nineteenth hole was what might be termed an unpardonable offence; and the error was all the more unexpected, as it was perpetrated by a man who has hardly ever failed at a critical moment. After the event many a man was heard to say, " I never saw Johnnie Ball do a thing like that before," and probably few ever had; but the slip was in a certain degree due to an error of judgment in the choice of the club, as previous to this shot he had been playing all his short approaches with a comparatively straight-faced club, and he could no doubt have successfully negotiated this pitch across the burn with the same club, but in an evil moment he took out his pitching mashie—a club he had hardly touched during the week's play.

A close analysis of the results in this championship would lead one to the belief that Leslie Balfour-Melville was somewhat lucky to win, as all of his last three heats were won on the nineteenth green, and on each occasion his success at this particular hole was chiefly due to mistakes on the part of his opponents. On the first occasion William Greig obligingly placed his second into the burn; on occasion number two, Laurence Auchterlonie was equally obliging, and the narrow strip of water did not fail to come to the winner's aid in the final round. Still this is all in the game, and there could be no doubt that he played up most pluckily on every occasion, and it is pluck as much as ability that wins championships.

My own participation in the open event that year, also played at St. Andrews, may be dismissed in a very few lines. In the first round I seemed to play against the wind all the way round, and as the men playing just behind me and just in front of me confirmed this opinion, I am justified in thinking that this assumption was not all pure imagination. Another fact impressed upon my memory is that we played the seventeenth hole in a hailstorm, and that in the month of June. In addition to these adverse climatic conditions, it must be truthfully added, that from a playing point of view I was not making at all good weather of it—a fact which filled my caddie with the most evident disgust, which he did not take the slightest pains to hide. The *finale* came at the sixteenth hole. A friend shouted out to me, "How are you getting on?" Before I could reply, my faithful henchman had grasped the opportunity of giving his idea of the situation. It was as follows: "Not o'er weel, at any rate; we're playing domd badly." I certainly could not refute the statement; it was very, very true.

This championship supplied one of Sandy Herd's numerous disappointments. He was leading at the end of the second round, and also at the end of the third round—three strokes dividing his score from that of Taylor, who lay second. In the afternoon there was a sudden change of weather—first the wind began to blow and then the rain came down. Herd played the first few holes without much rain, and made an excellent start; but then the elements began to play ducks and drakes with his game. He kept dropping strokes at nearly every hole, until he eventually took as many as 85. Still he had far from lost the championship, as it was not at all an easy day. Taylor had to face some of the worst of the weather in the first few holes played, and at the fourth hole he had dropped two more strokes to Herd; then the weather improved a little, and he fairly got going. That the effect of the rain was beneficial to his play was evident, as the saturated turf enabled him to pitch his iron shots up to the pin, and also allowed him to ram his putts at the back of the hole, both forms of the game to which he is very partial. And he did putt too, not actually phenomenally, but never a mistake—down in two every time. A few holes from home he had the championship literally in safe keeping; he made no mistake thereafter, and won easily.

It has always been generally considered that the rain saved Taylor that day, and perhaps there is some truth in the contention, as there can be but little doubt that once he felt that he could play boldly at the hole, he played with infinitely greater confidence than he had been doing on the hard and slippery turf. Again, Herd is a stamp of putter who likes a keen putting green. He trickles his putts, and in the final round he could not get up to the hole, being short in his approach putts time after time. Sandy has never been very lucky in championships.

During the winter I took the opportunity of giving my injured wrist a good rest, as for three months I never touched a club, and when I began to play again I quickly realised the wisdom of this act. I was still very chary about playing forcing shots from bad lies, and when playing them could not get away from the habit of letting go my left hand; it had gradually become a species of second nature. The championship at Sandwich, however, supplied me with a really good and severe test. The programme at Sandwich is always slightly more trying than that on other championship greens, owing to the competition for the St. George's Vase, which from the St. George's tees is a severe trial. In the championship I was distinctly favoured in the draw; in fact, this said draw at Sandwich was one of the most unequal in the history of the championship, as in the top half there were heaps of celebrities, whilst in the bottom half there were but few, and fortunately I happened to be in the bottom half. As it happened I went on winning my rounds, and in each succeeding round I found that my wrist seemed to gain strength, and this greatly added to my confidence. So I played on boldly as if nothing was the matter with my wrist, and although I occasionally felt a nasty jar I still persevered, and the farther I went the less I felt the injury.

One round in the earlier stages I shall always remember ; it was the round in which I had to meet H. S. Colt, and it was played in the morning of the day when the memorable storm swept down upon Sandwich like an avalanche. It was the most remarkable change of weather I have ever experienced ; the early morning supplied quite good golfing weather, but about twelve o'clock there was an ominous appearance in the sky. Something was coming was very evident, as the sky was as black as ink, but I think few were quite prepared for what did come. Without a moment's notice the wind swept down the course carrying everything before it and almost instantaneously flattening down the press and other tents.

At the time this little episode occurred I happened to be addressing my ball going to the tenth hole, played down wind. I managed to hit my ball into the air, but the weight of the wind soon brought it to mother earth. The last I saw of it for some time was a white object careering over the mounds like a feather. My opponent was nearly blown on his face, and just managed to scramble the ball off the tee, but the wind carried it on a considerable distance. Then we hurried to the best shelter we could obtain, and with the aid of my opponent's umbrella, which fortunately was of the tent-like variety, we guarded ourselves from the elements for something like twenty minutes or half-an-hour. When the unwelcome visitation had passed over, we proceeded to find the balls; his was easily found, but mine was not so easy to discover. Eventually we found it tucked up hard against the face of the pot bunker, lying to the left of the big bunker which has to be crossed with the second shot. It must have been over 300 yards from the tee, and yet that ball could not have carried over 100 yards. The force of the wind in that storm must have been extraordinary. I never got out of that bunker; my hands were so cold I could not hold my club. The play for the remainder of the round approached the farcical. We were both so cold that we could hardly hit the ball at all. At first my opponent had the best of this farce, and from being one down stood two up with five to play; then the pendulum swung round the other way. I squared the match, and eventually scrambled home on the twentieth green, where I had none the worst of the luck, as my tee shot, had it been straight, would certainly have been in the second bunker guarding the green; fortunately, however, it just skirted the right-hand edge, and finished some ten yards beyond, a fact which will give an idea as to the strength of the wind.

I got through to the penultimate round, and then had to meet John Graham, jun., whom many termed the Hoylake novice. I was not at all comfortable about the result,

as I knew well what the said youth could do.
People kept saying to me that he was sure
to break down, but I was not at all sure about
it; in fact I held the contrary opinion, that he
was little likely to do so. He can hardly be
said to have broken down, but it is true that
he did not play quite the game he had been
playing, his putting being particularly at fault,
and I got through somewhat easily.

In the final I received gruelling number three
from Freddie Tait. He was in a most merciless
mood, and I never had a chance. Not that I
was playing even indifferent golf, far from it, but
the truth was simply that I was outplayed in
every department of the game. Indeed there can
be but little doubt that this championship was
the one great particular triumph in Freddie
Tait's career. To begin with, he had won the
St. George's Vase, and in the championship too
he displayed extraordinarily fine form; his win
was all the more meritorious on account of the
fact that he had an exceptionally severe position
in the draw, as in succession he had to meet
Charles Hutchings, Laidlay, John Ball, jun.,

Horace Hutchinson, and the writer. He won four of these heats very easily, and only once was he in any way hustled, and that was against Horace Hutchinson in the semi-final round, when he was down on the way out. I remember one of his keenest supporters coming back to our match behind, and in a most tragic voice remarking, "Oh my Lord, I believe Freddie's funking; he's playing like a child." He, however, threw this childish fit aside and won comfortably. On a strict analysis of results I have always considered this win of his at Sandwich the finest ever accomplished in the championship, the only two to compare with it for ease being the win of John Ball, jun., in 1890 at Hoylake, and that of the writer at Sandwich in 1900, but in both instances the individual opposition to be overcome was not nearly so strong.

The Open Championship was that year played at Muirfield. Personally I had little to say in the matter. I simply played four rounds of a very indifferent character, the only item of interest in them being the fact that in each of them I took the same number of strokes to come home, and in three of them the same number of strokes to go out. I would rather not mention the figures.

It was a championship which heralded the coming of Harry Vardon. Previous to the contest there were probably a few who knew what a really fine player he was, and amongst those few must be included Taylor. He knew all about it, as just previous to the championship the fact had been very clearly impressed upon him in a match played at Ganton, when Harry fairly walked over him to the tune of something like eight up and six to play. Still his chance was not seriously considered by the majority, as was proved by the very few people who took the trouble to watch his play. It was once again the old couple Taylor and Herd who drew the crowd, and when the redoubtable Sandy led off with a round of 72, every one immediately remarked that his time had come at last, but he fell away terribly in the second round, taking over 80. Still he and Taylor were leading the field at the end of the day's play, and it looked

like a duel as in the previous year at St. Andrews.
In round number three Harry Vardon drew a
little nearer to the duellists. Still the public
never really considered his chance of success as
at all a likely one, and the spectators still left
him to play unattended. Taylor, who was an
early starter, finished in a steady 80—a score
which, whilst not making him at all safe, gave
him a total which would require some beating.
Herd was a very late starter, whilst Harry
Vardon was sandwiched in between them. That
day Vardon had been playing with James
Kinnell, and the latter decided to retire after
the first round. I happened to be playing with
old Tom, who for once in a way had departed
from his usual custom of retiring after the first
day's play. This extra round proved too much
for him, and he retired in consequence. I was
asked to play with Vardon in the fourth round,
and I readily acquiesced. When we had gone
some way round we heard that Taylor had
finished in 80, leaving Harry a total of 77 to
tie with him. It was a score which did not

allow for many mistakes, but Harry was always just there or thereabouts. Occasionally he got behind schedule, but promptly picked up the necessary stroke again. Even if he did tie with Taylor, however, or even beat him, there was always Herd to reckon with. As it so happened, when we were playing the fifteenth hole we met Herd's crowd coming up to the fourth, and what was more, we saw Herd hacking away in a big bunch of star grass on the edge of the bunker which divides the two courses. Whether this sight did Harry good or not I cannot say, but I do know that he promptly holed a mighty useful putt—a putt which made all the difference in the world; it left him a total of 14 strokes for the last three holes to tie, and there is a big difference between 13 and 14 for those last three holes at Muirfield. He did them in 14, playing carefully, and taking no undue risks. Poor Herd never got over that disaster at the fourth hole, and was out of it some way from home. Harry Vardon won the play off, and won his first championship.

Now to give an idea as to what extent his chance was esteemed by the general run of the spectators, it may be mentioned that we started that last round without a single individual watching. Eventually one casual spectator strolled up and followed us for a few holes, and finally asked me who I was playing with. When I told him, he didn't seem very much enlightened or impressed and eventually left us. Going to the twelfth hole, three or four of Taylor's crowd joined us, the remainder going off with Herd, who was just starting. When we met Herd's crowd, a friend asked me, "How is your man going?" I replied, "He is just about going to win." My friend joined the gradually increasing army, and eventually Harry Vardon, the ultimate winner, had ten spectators to see him play the last hole; had we not met Herd's crowd I doubt whether there would have been more than four. It seems absurd, but it is true. I know we played the sixth, seventh, eighth, ninth, tenth, and eleventh holes without a single spectator.

Before passing away from this championship a reference must be made to Freddie Tait. At Sandwich he had proved himself to be incomparably the best amateur golfer of the year, and at Muirfield he quite upheld this reputation; he made a gallant fight on the last day, and always maintained that but for bad luck he would have tied with Vardon and Taylor. I cannot say what happened before he played the sixteenth hole, but going to that hole he had to do an average of fours to tie—a pretty tall order, particularly as the sixteenth green was then quite new and very uneven, and it was this green which certainly did away with any chance that he had. His third was some eight yards from the hole. His putt seemed to be hit quite truly, but when about half-way to the hole it struck some obstruction; this took all the pace off the ball, and it stopped a good two yards short of the hole, from which distance he failed to hole out. Had he holed this putt he would have had left a total of seven for the last two holes. Of course the seventeenth is a very

G

possible three, and it was far from beyond his powers to reach the last green in two, but it is a charitable conclusion to think that that rub on the sixteenth green lost him the chance of playing off with Vardon and Taylor.

CHAPTER V

AFTER three years of comparatively profitless work came one which resulted in a rich and plentiful harvest. This was 1897 ; and although there may have been seasons in which I have played golf of an equally good character, still this year of 1897 is the one above any other year in which I turned my good play to account. Apart from a bad failure in the Amateur Championship, I managed to prove successful in nearly every event I took part in, including the Open Championship at Hoylake.

The Amateur Championship that year at Muirfield will always be remembered as "the championship of surprises." The big men went down one after another like ninepins. First Laidlay succumbed on the twentieth green to quite an unknown player, then Greig proved too much for

Freddie Tait, and John Ball, jun., had to depart on the twenty-third green. His defeat, however, was a distinctly honourable one, as, in the first place, his opponent was Robert Maxwell, and then, to aid this young gentleman's natural golfing ability, he had Sayers as a mentor, and this meant much to an inexperienced player, particularly over Muirfield, which Sayers knew well. To my mind that match was one of the finest I have ever seen in the history of the championship, the play in the extra five holes being far above what is usually seen on these trying occasions.

I was left to try and avenge the defeat of my club-mate at the hands of Maxwell, and a sorry effort I made. There was no excuse for my failure, as in preliminary practice I had been playing well, but in the previous heat it had become very evident to my inner consciousness that I was playing very jumpily, and that a little of my former confidence had disappeared. Still I trusted that it was but a very temporary lapse. Unfortunately it proved a very lasting lapse, as after accomplishing one very useful feat at the first hole, where I ran down a long putt for the hole, I never did anything even worthy of the faintest praise. For the remainder of the match it is true that I was accorded a very varied experience in the matter of manipulating stymies, none of which, by the way, I succeeded in overcoming; but not by the most egotistical stretch of imagination can I think that it made any difference in the result. As Freddie Tait would say, "I could play none." And what is more, for the rest of the week my golf was of a similarly helpless nature; in one match in which I partnered John Ball, jun., against Freddie Tait and Jack Graham— the game being a four-ball match—not on one single occasion was I of any assistance to my partner. I couldn't drive, I couldn't approach, nor could I putt. Still, *we* won that match.

To return to the championship. Maxwell was naturally a very strong favourite. After these somewhat untoward events, everything depended upon whether his nerve would stand the strain. Personally I think it broke a little, as against James Robb he did not play quite the same consistent game that he had done previously, and, moreover, did not appear so confident in himself. But Robb was playing a very fine game at that meeting.

In the meanwhile there was a young player named Allan unostentatiously working his way through; he was not knocking out Taits, Balls, or Laidlays, but what he had to do he was doing well. He had faithful adherents, who predicted his ultimate success; and one golfer, Mr. David Scott Duncan, the editor of the *Golfing Annual*, confidently told me before the event began that Allan would just about win.

At the time I didn't pay much attention to the prophecy, but it was brought home to me afterwards. When watching Allan play, one found it almost impossible to believe that he could work his way through such a good field, even granting that so many good men had been removed from his pathway, as his style was neither orthodox nor elegant, and he seemed to lack the true golfer's methods and finish. Still he got there, and in getting there never exhibited any of those numerous signs which tend to show that a player is either anxious or nervous. He might have been playing an ordinary game for the humble half-crown. In the penultimate round he had to meet Leslie Balfour-Melville, who by this time was becoming a decided favourite, and many a man was heard to say, "Old Leslie is going to win again—you'll see." But old Leslie could not get away from the young student, and at the fourteenth hole he was one down.

I shall never forget the tee shots to that hole. It was a distinctly difficult tee shot, as it is always narrow, and on this occasion there was a difficult head - wind to contend against. Allan had the honour, and hooked his ball into the bunker on the left-hand side of the course. Now was his opponent's opportunity, and by the time he took it was evident that he did not mean to leave anything to chance. He tried several tees before deciding on a suitable one; and then, through an interruption on the part of a spectator, stopped in the middle of his address to the ball and recommenced once again. Finally he hit it, and oh, what a shot—hard on the top—the ball gently rolling on until it finished in some loose sand in very close proximity to some sleepers. This fatal error literally lost him the match.

The other semi-final between Robb and John Low supplied an excellent example of the latter's match-playing abilities. Robb was dormie three, but Johnnie Low halved the match. He lost it ultimately on the twenty-first green, but Robb was lucky, as he badly hooked every one of his three tee shots, and on any course but Muirfield would probably have been punished by the loss of the hole and the match. His first tee shot struck the wall hard and bounded back into the course; his second many considered had gone over the wall, but luck was with him once again, and it was found on the right side. Again, at the third attempt, his ball finished perilously near the wall, but he obtained a sufficiently good lie to take a wooden club, and he put his second on the green and won the hole. Any one of those tee shots should have lost him the match.

The final round was far from a brilliant affair, and was unfortunately marred by an incident which is often discussed to this day. It was the wall incident at the eleventh hole in the second round, and to put the case succinctly it may be said that Allan hooked his second shot hard against the wall, from which it rebounded, and the ball could not be found ; eventually it was found in the pocket of Robb's caddie, who either wilfully or in a fit of mental aberration had picked it up. James Robb, his employer, had nothing to do with the incident, but had to pay the penalty—the loss of the hole—and this may have made a big difference in the game. It was distinctly hard lines on Robb, as it left his opponent three up, with only six holes to play, and moreover probably had a demoralising effect on Robb's game for the remaining holes.

Poor Jack Allan died early in the following year, and the golfing world were never granted an opportunity of forming a decided opinion as to whether his success was as much due to fortune as many critics averred that it was. That he was a wonderful putter there can be no doubt whatever, and moreover he appeared a wonderful judge of distance; his game certainly lacked variety, and in consequence was not so attractive as that of many well-known players, but his friends believe in him to this day, and always put him on the exalted pedestal which by right belongs to a great golfer.

1897 was the first year in which an Open Championship was played at Hoylake, and the local element looked forward very confidently to one or other of the Royal Liverpool men upholding the prestige of Hoylake golf. Perhaps there was a little justification for the belief, as on the two previous occasions on which the amateur event had been held on the Cheshire green, Johnnie Ball had wiped out all opposition, and although I had personally failed on these two occasions, there was a deep-rooted conviction, right or wrong, that I was about half a stroke a hole a better player in score-playing than in match-playing, and the majority put away from their mind my many failings in the field of personal antagonism. Time after time people came to me and remarked, " Johnnie and you ought to have a great chance this year." Personally I thought there was a slight chance of one or other of the twain making a good fight, but I had seen a good deal of professional golf, and the more I saw of it the more did I respect its many qualities. Local knowledge may be a distinct asset, but I came to the conclusion that we wanted all that and a little more to get in front of Taylor, Herd, Vardon, Braid, and company. The lesson taught in 1894, 1895, and 1896 had not been lost upon me, and it was evident that the professional was gradually leaving the amateur behind, and the latter would have to hurry up if he wished to get his nose in front again.

Round number one ended in nothing very sensational; 78, I believe, was the best round, and there were numerous players within a few strokes of this total. For my own part, I finished in 80, and might have done better but for having to play behind the crowd which followed Johnnie Ball and Laidlay, who were immediately in front of me. Time after time we had to wait until they cleared away from the greens, and going to the sixteenth hole we had to wait fully ten minutes, as the crowd remained right in the line of play until the said couple had played their second shots to the seventeenth. From their own point of view the spectators were probably wise, as by moving a few yards they could not only see the sixteenth hole played out, but moreover see the tee shots and second shots played to the seventeenth hole; but it was very exasperating to those behind, and I know I was very irritable about it. In round number two I decided to keep well behind them, and did so with happy results, as with one hole to play I had a four for 75. A four to this hole I did not expect, as it was played dead against the wind, and it was quite impossible to get home in two. A five would have quite satisfied me. When I had played my approach my ball lay about four yards from the hole. I was standing by the ball whilst my partner was playing a long approach putt, and Mr. Ryder Richardson, who was holding the pin, remarked, " Did you hear what Braid has done ? " I said, " No ; " he replied, " Seventy-four." This took my breath away, but at the same time probably did me good, as I went boldly for the hole and holed the putt, and they wanted holing on that green, as many found out. In the end that putt meant much.

At the end of the day's play Braid was leading with a total of 154, while I was second with a total of 155, with Freddie Tait, Johnnie Ball, Pulford, and Herd close behind. Round number three is in my opinion always a most crucial one in a championship, particularly to a man who is occupying a position which gives him a chance

of success.   It is probably the most testing
round of the whole four.   When I won the
championship at Muirfield it was my third
round of 72 which literally won me that
championship, for it lifted me up about a dozen
places in the list.   In my third round at
Hoylake I did my best to throw the championship into the gutter, as whilst I was making no
serious mistakes, I played the most weak-kneed
golf.   I cannot remember touching a single
hazard, and still I took no less than 84; it was
simply that I would not hit the ball up to the
hole, with the result that at literally every other
hole I dropped a stroke.   My partner, Peter
Paxton, did his best to comfort me, but his
sympathy was of no avail, and I went to lunch
a very sick and peevish man, the only grain
of comfort I could derive being the fact that
Braid had also failed and taken 82.   The others
of course had crept up, and I found that I was
relegated from second to fifth position.   I cannot say that this affected my lunch, as on top
of many good things I finished up with some

trifle, simply on the recommendation of an individual not unassociated with the inner management of the Royal Liverpool Club, who confidently asserted that it was the finest thing in the world on which to do a 75—as events turned out, one of the truest things he has said in this world.

When I arrived on the tee my old friend Paxton greeted me with the remark, "Now, Mr. Hilton, a 75 this afternoon, nothing more." The number 75 seemed to be in the air. The start was very auspicious, as a putt of fifteen to twenty yards found the bottom, and a three was placed on the card; a four came at the second, and then there came a shot which might have ended in serious disaster. In the three previous rounds the wind had been nearly dead behind the players, and it had been necessary to play very carefully to remain short of the bunker. I had noticed, however, that the wind had been gradually changing, and instead of being behind, was inclined to be across. First I addressed the ball with my spoon, and then changed my mind and took a longer club to get as near the bunker as possible. Just as I was addressing the ball my caddie, who was becoming a little excited, remarked, "Take care; you will get in with that." I simply remarked, "Will you shut up?"—not very courteous certainly, but I did know the Hoylake links. The result of the shot was disastrous, as I cut across it, and it pitched right into a little bunker beside the "Field" green. I saw the sand fly up. When I arrived on the scene I found fortune on my side, as the ball had pitched in the bunker, and in so doing had thrown up a little mound of sand on which the ball was perched, the only difficulty being that there was a bank in front of me. I decided, however, to go for it, and taking my spoon I played for a hook, brought the shot off and holed out in five. A very useful two followed at the next hole, and a four was quite satisfactory at the fifth hole. A total of 18 for the first five holes was more than satisfactory, and I had no ambition to play them over again. When, however, one starts in this sensational fashion, and then has a little time to deliberate upon the question of possibilities, as one invariably has in a big field in the Open Championship, thoughts and fancies pass through the mind, and these thoughts and fancies are apt to upset the equilibrium of the most staid of players. Whether this happened in my case or not I cannot say, but there is one thing certain, and that is that for a short spell I tried my best to discount this great start, and began to play the fool on the green at the very next hole. As my second shot left me but a few yards from the pin, I promptly putted short, and followed this up by missing a very short one. The seventh or " Dowie " hole is always a trying one, and it has always been a hole which I have had reason to remember as an enemy, nor on this occasion did it prove any exception to the rule. In the three previous rounds I had played it a little too safely, and on each occasion had taken four to it. On the present occasion I determined to play boldly

H

for the green, with the result that I held the ball too much into the wind and it just pitched out of bounds. Number two was more successful, as it finished close to the hole; but once again three putts were required, and I began to realise that I was gradually dissipating a glorious chance. A five to the eighth was quite satisfactory, but another stroke went astray at the ninth, as once again three strokes were required on the green; I found myself therefore with a total of 38 for the outward journey, and at one time I had had dreams and visions of 36 or something under that figure. And, what was worse, the harder part of the journey had to be overcome, for a great deal of this journey had to be played against a head-wind.

Whilst standing on the tee to the tenth, I heard that Freddie Tait was also out in 38, which was not at all comforting news, as it meant that he still held a lead of one stroke. I always consider that the first four holes home on the Hoylake course are exceedingly crucial ones in a medal round. They comprise that portion of the course where it is either possible for a man to pull himself together and transform an average beginning into quite a respectable score, or back up a good outward journey in such a fashion that except for extreme disaster in the last five holes, a good total is ensured. Now, fortunately for me, I got those holes in schedule numbers, viz., four, three, four, three. In doing so I had one piece of good fortune, in that at the eleventh, or "Alps" hole, I laid a short pitch from the top of the hill literally stone dead. This little help brought my score down to an average of fours. The "Field" hole was a trying one that day, and I was very thankful to leave it in the rear with an orthodox five. Then came a little bit of fortune which was extremely useful, as at the "Lake" hole I ran down a very useful putt for a four, and I knew well that at this stage every stroke must make a difference. This gave me heart of grace, and I played the "Dun" hole confidently, and this notwithstanding that I had to wait a very long time before I could

play my second shot; but I had my nerves
well in control, and was determined not to be
bustled, and I did not strike until the course
in front was absolutely clear of spectators.
Down in five I was left with a four and a five
for 75; but the five came first, as I was
terribly short both with my approach and my
approach putt to the seventeenth, and missed
my fourth.

Now in the three previous rounds it was
literally an impossibility for me to reach the
last green in two, but I had noticed during
the round that the wind had been gradually
whipping round from the east to the north, and
in place of being almost dead ahead at this
hole, it was now almost directly across the line
of the hole; in consequence I decided to have
a go at my tee shot in the hope that I might
get over in two. I had a go, and got fairly
hold of the ball, but when I came up to it I
found that, notwithstanding that I had really
hit the shot, there were still grave doubts as to
whether I could get home. My caddie handed

me a club with which to play short, but I had
a good look at it, and decided to have a dash
at it. I had plenty of time in which to weigh
up the pros and cons of the situation, for the
couple in front seemed to be playing some kind
of game of their own on the green; they may,
in fact, have been not at all slow, but to me
it seemed an interminable time. I badly wanted
to get this shot over, as the more I looked at
it the less I liked it. At last came the welcome
signal, and without wasting any time over pre-
liminaries I let go. The ball went as true as steel
off the club, but unfortunately I had the slightest
bit of pull on the stroke, and I knew well
that the farther you go to the left at this hole
the longer is the carry.

Directly they saw the ball sail away from the
club, the spectators began to cheer and clap;
they promptly took it for granted that it must
clear the bunker, but I knew that it was a
case of touch and go. I had played that
hole far too often, and in my anxiety I mentally
stigmatised them as fools for their somewhat

premature applause. I should not have been at all surprised had the ball plumped straight into the bunker, but it got over, by how much I cannot say; I have an idea that it must have been more a question of feet than yards, as by the way it jumped it must have landed on the bank just over the hazard; but "all's well that ends well," and it was over and close to the hole. Putt number one was not at all a bold one. One spectator called it a drunken effort, and he was not far wrong. Putt number two dobbled about, and eventually made its entry into the hole at the back door, but it got there, and that was everything. I can see that ball now hesitating on the lip of the hole like a helpless derelict.

In the meanwhile I had heard that Freddie Tait had come to grief on the way home, in fact I was aware of that a hole or two from home. How many people took the trouble to tell me of it I do not know, but they were certainly a goodly number, as during the intervals of waiting they came trooping up one after another, no doubt with the very best of intentions, though I was by degrees becoming a little tired of the same information. My chief enemy I knew to be James Braid, and almost immediately after I had finished it was somewhat pleasing to hear that he had commenced his round very indifferently, and that it was more than probable that he would require more than 40 for the outward journey; as he required a total of 77 for the round to supplant my aggregate score, and a total of 78 to tie, I felt fairly confident as to the result, particularly as the homeward half had to be played against the wind. After a short rest I thought I should like to go out and see mine enemy finish. I wandered forth and met him coming to the twelfth hole. I saw him play his second shot to that hole, and a fine straight shot it was, dead on the pin, but a little strong. On it trickled until it disappeared over the ridge which guards the pond beyond the hole; personally I thought it had found a watery grave, but on investigation I found that it had not reached the water. Still, the fact did not trouble me much. I was buoyed up by the rumour of the indifferent commencement of his round. This rumour proved to be quite correct; his start for that fourth round was very inauspicious, but the probability that he would require more than 40 for the outward journey did not materialise, for he holed those nine holes in 40, and what was worse, began the homeward half with a four and a three. This information came to me from a spectator who apparently did not realise my identity, as in reply to my query as to how Braid was doing, he remarked, " He's making a great fight of it against Hilton; he's out in 40, and has started home with a four and a three." I felt inclined to say, " Thank you for very unpleasant news." My equanimity of spirit promptly faded away. I began to anxiously reckon what he had to do to either win or tie, and the more I reckoned the less I liked the situation; but I thought, " At any rate I will see the show out like a brave man, and watch him finish." I quickly found out, however, that my mental stamina was not quite equal to the strain, and after seeing him play two holes I had had quite enough of it, and I thought to myself, "Young man, this is no place for you," and then there was one spectator the less in that crowd. It really was trying to see James Braid trying to hole putts and miss them by a hair's-breadth. Both at the twelfth hole I have mentioned, and again at the "Rushes," it was touch and go whether the ball went in or not. As it happened the ball didn't, the spectators murmured "Hard lines," and I murmured "Thank heaven," and wandered away to the clubhouse and tried to take an intelligent interest in the newspapers. I was sitting there in complete solitude until joined by a near relative, who at first said nothing, but sat down a short distance away; eventually he sympathetically remarked, "You must not be disappointed if you do not win; that man Braid is a very fine player." I naturally came to the conclusion that Braid must have done something out of the common at the "Field" hole, and events proved that my surmise was correct, as he had holed it in four against the wind, and that made a big difference. I didn't make any inquiries as to details, however, but to relieve my feelings went into the billiard-room and tried to play a game with a kindly friend, who sacrificed himself on my behalf. I cannot think that I took much interest in that game, for I was soon at the club window watching the enemy playing the sixteenth hole, and I cannot say I was sorry to see him take six for the hole. Looking from the window I could not make much of the proceedings to the seventeenth, but the hole took so long to play that I came to the conclusion that the total was more likely to be five than four, and I summoned up enough pluck to wander out again to see the finish, and the first thing I heard was a shout, " He's a three to tie." I felt quite a brave man again, as I knew that last hole at Hoylake. It is always a good four, and an exceptional three, and, moreover, on this occasion there were one or two reasons which made it all the more difficult. Firstly, the wind was if anything against the player; not that this would stop Braid from getting home in two, but it necessitated a long approach in place of a short one. Again, the hole was placed in a most difficult position. Mr. Ryder Richardson told me that he had never seen such terrible putting in his life as he had at this hole. Nearly every one had been skating about round the hole like small children, and he had hardly seen a decent putt holed during the whole of the two days' play.

In my own mind I could not see Braid or any one else doing that hole in three, and I felt that the championship was in my pocket. I had an anxious moment or two, however. To begin with, his drive was one of the best, and it was very evident that he could easily get home in two. First he took out a wooden club, then hesitated and walked some distance forward, and eventually decided to take an iron one. In James Braid's long career he has probably seldom played a finer stroke than that second of his to this last hole in 1897; it was never off the pin. Everything depended upon the roll of the ball. On it came, and nobody could accurately tell where it would stop. Fortunately for me the green was keen, and it kept trickling along, passed within a foot or so of the hole, and did not stop until it had rolled some six or eight yards past. As befitted the occasion, he took any amount of pains over that putt; but, personally, I felt very confident as to the result. I knew that hole and its position, and, moreover, the putt was a difficult one. He made an excellent bid, but the ball skidded past on the left-hand side, and I once again said, "Thank heaven." From a mere question of distance that putt was a very holeable one, but I had a good look at it, and I don't think he would have holed it once in ten minutes, as there was a swing away from the hole on both sides; besides that it was one of those holes cut in such a manner, or perhaps placed in such a position, that few putts found the bottom thereof, unless they hit the back of the hole fair and square. As I have said before, my personal knowledge of that particular hole greatly added to my confidence when Jimmie Braid attempted to hole that fateful third stroke.

I remember, when afterwards discussing the championship, a friend remarked to me, "You *must* have been in a blue funk when Braid was playing that putt of his to tie." I assured him that such was far from the case, as I felt in a much more composed state than I had done for some considerable time previously. He would not believe me, however, and apparently considered that my suggestion that at the moment I was not suffering from the nervousness of fear and anxiety arose more from the promptings of the *after* thoughts, than those of truth. Nevertheless it was the truth, and nothing but the truth; and although a certain qualm of nervousness came over me when I realised that he had hit the ball absolutely truly—a thing which in those days Braid was not very wont to do—still this qualm was very short-lived, for standing behind him, I quickly realised that the ball was bearing away to the left-hand side of the hole, and little short of a miracle would enable it to reach its proposed destination. Possibly to the spectators standing across the line of the putt it may have seemed a very near thing indeed, and from a spectator's point of view so it was, as the ball was struck quite correctly; it had just sufficient strength to carry it past the hole, and when it had travelled half-way it was extremely doubtful where it would finish. But to any observant person who was standing behind the striker, it was evident that once the ball began to near the hole it must pass on the left-hand side, although there can be but little doubt that it was a very fine effort to hole an extremely difficult putt.

Of all my championship successes, I have always looked back upon this particular one at Hoylake with the greatest degree of satisfaction. It is true that I had previously won a championship, but that was five years previously, and it was won under somewhat peculiar conditions. In the first place, the course at Muirfield, for many reasons, could not be considered a truly severe test of the game, as in addition to its extreme shortness there was far too much of the drive and pitch variety of hole in evidence, and in those days pitching was certainly the most deadly part of my game. Again, on the concluding day I had an absolute day out. It would not be perhaps correct to say that everything came off—such a state of affairs can hardly be expected in two rounds of eighteen holes; but it is true that very little went wrong, and if I did make a slight mistake, it seldom cost me anything. Now between this year of 1892 and the championship of 1897 I had done very little, at least in the big events, and this tended to confirm those who considered that this win at Muirfield was very much of the nature of a fluke. In consequence it is easy to understand that an endorsement of the previous win was particularly gratifying to me, even though in this second success I had the advantage of playing over a course with which I was well acquainted. No doubt that did mean just a little at Hoylake in 1897, as the green was hard and burnt, and in consequence was as keen as a skating-rink.

CHAPTER VI

I⊤ may be imagination on my part, but I
have always considered that never during my
whole career have I played so consistently well
as in the earlier months of the year 1898, and
I say this notwithstanding the success which
fell to my share in 1897. Well as I played in
that year, I always look back upon the spring of
the following season as the high-water mark in
my golfing career; but there was the same old
story to tell, another disastrous failure, in the
Amateur Championship, and absolutely the worst
failure I had ever been guilty of. Even now
when I think it over I cannot find any excuse
for that humiliating exhibition in the fourth
round at Hoylake. It was sad and pitiful, but
more of this anon.

In Easter week that year the Royal Liverpool

Club took a team down to Westward Ho to play a return match with the Royal North Devon Club. The team was not the very strongest that the Hoylake club could turn out, but it was quite a good team, and I rather think that few of that combination anticipated defeat. Personally it never entered my head that we should be beaten; at least it never entered my head until I had an opportunity of gauging the value of the Southerners, and then it seemed to me that whilst they could not claim the services of any very noted men, there still was a uniformity in the form of the whole team which spelt danger for our tail end. The North Devon team was one of those combinations which you could almost turn upside down without making much material difference to the side. The first few men were no doubt better than the last three, but not to any appreciable extent, whilst on the other hand there must have been about half a stroke difference in the form of the best and the worst of our team. As events turned out, my premonition of disaster proved only too correct, as our tail let us down badly, and we were unexpectedly beaten. Still, from a personal point of view I had no reason to look back upon the match with any feelings of dissatisfaction, as I subscribed thirteen holes to the Royal Liverpool total, and in the subsequent play during the meeting won the "Kashmir" Cup by a margin of seven strokes, and also the Gold Medal with a score of 79, accomplished in half a gale of wind. This was certainly one of the best individual rounds I have ever played in my life, as is proved by the fact that the next scratch score to mine was that of John Ball, jun., 87; and moreover, notwithstanding a penalty of nine strokes, I finished first in the handicap list. Sad to say, I had refused to enter for the sweepstake, and as I was not eligible for the prize, all that remained was honour and glory. Following on this there was an open meeting at St. Anne's, and I won the scratch prize by no less than twelve strokes. The recapitulation of these events may sound very egotistical, but I record them in order to show that there was no explanation for my exhibition in the championship except utter inability to surmount a difficult situation.

When the draw came out I quickly realised that I was in close proximity to my old enemy, Lieutenant F. G. Tait, and by a very simple process of calculation it was easy to see that in case we both survived we should once again meet in the fourth round on the afternoon of the second day. I reached that fourth round fairly easily, and in doing so quite kept up the form I had been showing. On the other hand, Master Freddie had a desperately near affair with Charles Hutchings. He eventually won, and I am not going to say that he did not deserve to win, as his enemy holed one or two right across the green, and how his ball kept out of the hole on the last green is a mystery; it was another one from a very long way off—a species of distance from which you would feel satisfied if you kept the ball dead, but twelve inches from the hole it looked down for a certainty, only to slip round the edge of the hole. True it is that Freddie Tait would have had a putt to halve the match, but it was a putt of many yards. Playing the nineteenth hole, he played one of the finest shots I have ever seen him play, as from a pulled tee shot he put his second from a distance of over 200 yards within a few yards of the hole, and his opponent obligingly missing his approach, Freddie qualified for this fateful fourth round.

Our meeting was generally accorded the credit of being *the* match of the week, a species of battle royal. People trooped out from Liverpool in hordes to witness it, and I shouldn't like to try to count how many people exhorted me to be sure and buck up. All I know is that by degrees I became a little tired of their well-meant sympathy, not to say a little irritable, particularly when a man came up a few minutes before the start and, taking me aside, requested me to put some money on for him. He seemed a little hurt when I told him he must have mistaken me for a commission agent. I had quite enough to think about without running round chasing prospective gamblers.

Well, the crowd was there all right, and what came they out for to see? In truth one of the biggest walk-overs ever seen on a golf course. The trouble commenced at the second hole. I actually had a putt for that hole, but eventually lost it. When waiting to play the tee shot to the third hole a man I never expected to see on the links at all came to me, gently smacked me on the back, and remarked, "How are you getting on?" This kindly attention, well meant no doubt, did not serve to allay my irritability, and I promptly missed that tee shot, and another hole went astray. So the game proceeded; my opponent gradually increased his lead, and increased it without an effort, until finally I was six holes in arrear, with only five to play, and in consequence was free to wend my sorrowful way to the clubhouse. And sorrowful I did feel; it was akin to the sorrow of shame, and I really felt as if I dare not look anybody in the face. Freddie Tait was very sympathetic, but I am afraid I was past appreciating sympathy. I was feeling far too much humiliated. For the rest of that meeting I spent a good deal of time answering the oft-repeated query, "Whatever was the matter with you, old fellow?" and eventually had recourse to the answer, "Please don't ask me."

Freddie Tait eventually won that championship, but it was just about the luckiest win in the whole of his career. I have already recounted his squeak against Charles Hutchings, but he had two others equally as close, and if John Graham, jun., could have holed the most infantile of putts, another name than that of Tait would have been inscribed upon the championship trophy for the year 1898; he missed them, however, and the one he missed on the last green was just about the shortest I have ever seen missed in a championship.

Again, any one who saw Tait's match against John Low in the penultimate round will hardly forget it. With the probable exception of the memorable final in the following year at Prestwick, when John Ball, jun., won on the thirty-seventh green, this match at Hoylake was the most exciting I have ever witnessed. Not that the golf was good, far from it ; but those matches in which there is a very grave doubt as to what the players will do next are infinitely more exciting to witness than the mechanical kind of procedure which the leading professionals so often oblige us with. This day happened to be one of Freddie's off days from the tee, and he didn't forget to supply the gallery with some weird examples of where a tee shot should not be placed. Towards the conclusion of the round he was all over the place, but as usual he managed to hang on to a man who was playing decidedly the sounder golf of the two. His greatest feat was at the sixteenth hole, where he drove into the ditch guarding the out-of-bounds enclosure. His second shot only got him out of this hazard with some ten or fifteen yards to spare, and then he proceeded to place his third on the green, a mere carry of about 200 yards. It was a great effort at a very critical moment. Eventually the round was halved, and the fun still continued in the play off. The first hole was halved, but the end seemed certain to come at the twentieth hole, as Freddie half topped his approach, and ran past the hole into the grip beyond. His third was again an indifferent one, leaving him some seven or eight yards away. In the meanwhile John Low placed his third dead, and this putt of seven or eight yards had to be sunk or all was over. Down it went, but I cannot help thinking that that putt was a lucky one, as he hardly took the trouble to look at it, a most unusual thing for him; he simply walked up and hit it. Another nasty obstacle overcome.

There were more, however, in the offing, as he pulled his next tee shot to square leg, and out of bounds it went, so that he had to drop another and lose one. John Low was eventually on the green in three, and everything depended upon Freddie's fourth, a full wooden club shot; it was well played, but always seemed to be working away to the right of the hole. When

it pitched, however, it got a most extraordinary
kick towards the pin, and finally finished up
but a few yards away, and down he ran his
putt once again. The finish came at the next
hole, where John Low failed in his putting
and his enemy did not. It really was a most
extraordinarily lucky win. In the final round
against Mure Fergusson his luck did not desert
him, as although he played sounder golf than on
the previous day, some of his recoveries, particularly towards the end of the first round, were
sufficient to break a heart of stone.

The Open Championship that year was held
at Prestwick, a course which, in my own opinion,
should suit my style of play better than any
other of the four courses on which the championship is played. Yet, notwithstanding this
opinion, it is a fact that I have won championships over St. Andrews, Hoylake, Sandwich, and
Muirfield, but never over the green of my
choice — Prestwick. But I came very near to
winning one in 1898, and I always look back
upon the event as the one occasion on which

I threw away a championship through the agency of one bad stroke. It was a bad stroke, a very bad one, but even so it hardly deserved the fate that was meted out to it.

Notwithstanding my egregious failure at Hoylake in the previous month, there were not lacking those who held the opinion that I had a decided chance of repeating my success of 1897, and one sporting journalist actually tipped me outright to win. I cannot say that the confidence in my own powers was sufficiently great to lead me to endorse this opinion, as I had not yet got over the terrible *débâcle* at Hoylake; but I had a wooden club with which I could literally place the ball where I liked, one of those clubs which one meets with but seldom in a lifetime, and on a course like Prestwick this means much; a good servant it was to me that year, as in the whole four rounds of the championship I never once found trouble from the tee.

It would be difficult to say that year who started favourite. Many pinned their faith to

Harry Vardon, whilst in Scotland there was more than a sincere hope that Willie Park would stem the tide of English success; there was every reason for this hope, as he had been in strict training for some time, and recently had beaten Willie Fernie in a home-and-home match by a majority which seemed absolutely silly against a man of Fernie's class. Park meant business that year, there was no doubt about it, and the business very nearly came off.

As it happened, I was one of the early starters on the first day, and I have a distinct recollection of beginning the round in a very nervous fashion, but this soon wore off, and I finished in 76. Park, who was a late starter, also commenced in a very scratchy way, and on his play might have taken a considerable number for the first three holes, but his putting came to the rescue, so that he actually holed out these three holes in a total of twelve. I did not see the rest of the round, but I was told that from that point he played good golf. He also finished in 76; and at the end of the round we were leading the field—Vardon's score, it may be mentioned, being 79. Round number two I commenced full of confidence, and by the time I had holed out the fourth hole I had a total two strokes better than that of my morning round; then came the disaster spoken of before. The "Himalayas," particularly with the aid of a slight wind, is not a very terrifying hole, in fact it is a very simple one to play. In the morning round I had taken an iron club, and was a few yards short of the green. In the afternoon round I came to the conclusion that a little more force was required, so I took out a driving mashie, which I had not touched for over six months; it was quite a good club, but just a little too long in the handle for me. The result was that I hit the ground, and pulled the ball round into the sand-hill on the left. I carefully watched the particular bunch of bent grass that it struck, and to this day I wish that I had not. Notwithstanding that I knew the exact locality of the ball, it took some time to find it, and had I not marked it carefully down I should almost to a certainty have lost it; that would have been very much to my advantage, as I could have come back to the tee and played three, with the possibility of obtaining a five—a figure which, as events turned out, would have been sufficient to give me the championship. Unhappily I found that ball, and a pretty place it was in; for a moment I hesitated whether I should take it out and tee it, losing two strokes, but there was literally no sound place on which to tee it, as the surroundings were one mass of sand. Eventually I decided to play it. Effort number one ended in the ball being driven farther into the bent; effort number two, played from a different position, sent the ball high into the air, and after some waiting it condescended to come down and bury itself in the sand, just the top being visible; effort number three loosened it from its sandy prison, and effort number four sent it on its way to the green, where, to end the tale of disaster, it eventually finished in a deep divot mark half way down the hill; a run up and two putts found the bottom of the hole, and the next words uttered came from the marker, "I think that is eight;" he knew it was eight, and so did I, but I appreciated his kindly suggestion that he only *thought* it was eight.

Whilst all this travail was proceeding I never once lost control of my feelings, but once it was over I relieved the tension by throwing my putter at the teeing-box; fortunately it pitched short and bounded over the object of my wrath. Suddenly I thought, "What a fool you are; if you had hit that teeing-box and smashed the club where would you have been, as you haven't got another putter with you?" and I then solemnly worked out the possibilities of the round, and came to the conclusion that I might yet finish in 80. I did not manage 80 but was very near it, as my total was 81. To make matters worse, Park did a 75 and so did Vardon, so I found myself a good many strokes in arrear when round number three came to be played.

On the second day I happened to be a comparatively late starter. Park and Vardon, who

were some couples in front of me, both did well.
If my memory serves me aright the former finished
in 78 and Vardon in 77. My own score was the
same as that of Vardon, viz., 77, but I did throw
away strokes on the putting greens. My marker, a
well-known Prestwick golfer, told me afterwards
that he could have kicked me, and if he had
done it I think I might have forgiven him.

With round number four to play it appeared as if
the championship rested between Park and Vardon,
and in the end such was the case. Vardon, who
was the first to finish, handed in a 76, making a
full total of 307. Park had a comparatively short
putt to tie, and missed it. It is said that at the
time he had an idea that the putt he missed
was to beat Vardon and not to tie with him,
but of this I know nothing; all I know is that
I was proceeding on my way in this said fourth
round in a very satisfactory manner. I had no
idea what Park and Vardon were doing, it was
sufficient for me to know that it was necessary
to go all the way, and I had no reason to
grumble at an outward total of 35. Even so

a little luck at the eighth and ninth holes might have saved me two strokes, as on each occasion the ball just ran round the hole; but in each case the shot was played from a very long distance away, and it would have been extraordinarily good luck had either of these shots gone down. Homeward I began with a five and a four, and a very useful four at the twelfth—the hole over the wall. Then it was that I first heard how the land lay. A spectator asked me how I was getting on. I replied that I was an average of fours, and after a rapid mathematical calculation he remarked, "You are level with Park and Vardon at this point." This was encouraging news, although I have always had my doubts whether it was very beneficial to my chance, as at the thirteenth I made a slip. It happened thus. My tee shot was a long one, but slightly pulled. I am told by those who had an opportunity of witnessing its course that I had more than an average degree of luck in missing the pot bunker on the left, as the ball ran over the corner of the hazard. Still, "all's

K

well that ends well," and I was in easy reach
of the green. The lie was a good one, but the
stance was not of the best, as I had perforce to
stand very much below the ball. In consequence,
I took my spoon to slice it into the wind. Just
as I was addressing the ball my caddie, who had
been asked little and had talked less, suddenly
became excited and remarked, " You will go too
far with that club." I said nothing but walked
away, and addressed the ball once again ; but the
result was not happy, as I spared the shot too
much and was very short, and took five to
hole out.

The fourteenth hole was an easy one that
day. and I had no difficulty in getting a four.
In the meanwhile I had no idea what my two
enemies were doing ; but I realised that every
stroke must tell, and, moreover, that a great
deal depended upon the fifteenth and sixteenth
holes, which had to be played against the wind.
My tee shot to the fifteenth was too much to
the right, and finished under the hill. Still I
could easily get home, but I could not see the

line of the hole, and eventually made a mistake by playing too much to the right, and finished below the green. Not getting my next dead, I had to be content with a five. I knew by this time that I had to do something desperate to the sixteenth. I played my tee shot well to the right, so as to give me as easy an approach as possible. I shall always remember that approach, as I thought I had played it to perfection. Just over the corner of the " Cardinal " bunker, it cleared the hazard all right, but failed to surmount the hill beyond, and rolled back into the pathway on loose sand, and another five was recorded. Then I heard that a three and a two were required to tie with Vardon. This statement, as events turned out, proved to be inaccurate, as a total of six would have sufficed. But it can hardly be said to have made the slightest difference, as although I nearly holed out the seventeenth in three, a miss is as good as a mile, and in any case the last hole is always a difficult three. As it happened I took four to this hole, and finished one stroke behind Park and two behind Vardon.

This championship is the one event in my career which I have always grudged another man winning. It was lost by one silly mistake — a mistake absolutely the result of over-confidence—and whilst it taught me a lesson, it was a lesson learnt at a very big cost. Had I not marked that ball at the fifth hole I should probably have lost it, and been able to go back to the tee and play three. Even had I decided to take the ball out and tee it, I should probably have holed out in six, and such a figure would have sufficed to tie with Vardon, but the fact remains that I took eight to that hole. And, in a way, I deserved to take eight, for, in the first place, I had no right to take a club about which I knew little; and, in the second, if there was any doubt I should certainly have taken my wooden spoon, as I knew then, as I know now, that I am much safer with a wooden club than with an iron one. When I talked over the event with the veteran,

Mr. William Doleman, he was, to put the case mildly, a little bit unsympathetic on the point, as he remarked, " It serves you right ; you don't deserve any sympathy. You have often expressed the opinion that in case of doubt it is always safer to take a wooden club, and you go and take an iron one." It was an opinion expressed by a golfer of great experience. I said nothing, but valued it all the more.

CHAPTER VII

THE Amateur Championship of 1899 will always remain in my memory as one of the most exciting I ever witnessed. To begin with, the entry was just about as good as it could be, for although the names of one or two men with a slight chance of success were missing, still this championship at Prestwick supplied the most representative entry that has ever taken part in the event. For my own part, I once again found myself not so very far away from Frederick Guthrie Tait, provided I survived the initial round. There was a fair margin for a little practice before I could meet him, as the draw decided that we should not meet until the fifth round. It so happened that it was by the merest chance we ever met at all, as I had a terribly narrow shave against John

Gairdner in the preceding heat. Indeed, I should have had no cause to grumble had I not survived, as I was twice in dire straits. To begin with, he was dormie one, and that last hole is a difficult hole to win from any one. Fortunately he missed two approaches running, and although I did succeed in placing my own approach stone dead, I do not claim much credit for the feat, as a stroke placed a few yards farther away would have sufficed quite as well. I cannot say, moreover, that I actually tried to put that shot very very near the hole. I was quite satisfied to place it within holing distance, for my antagonist was still twenty yards from the hole and had already played three. In the second place, I proceeded to the tee to the nineteenth hole, and played out for a pull, foolishly I think; the pull did not come off, with the result that the ball sailed away into the railway. My opponent made no mistake with his drive, as it was right down the middle of the course. There was a rule then at Prestwick that in case of driving into the railway a ball should be dropped at the spot at which it crossed the dyke, under a penalty of one stroke. Well, the question arose as to the exact spot at which my ball had crossed, and a well-known member of the Prestwick Club settled the question for us. Being across the line of the flight of the ball, he could arrive at a fair conclusion, and had no hesitation in giving his decision. I simply mention this question as there were many arguments afterwards as to the correctness of his decision, some expressing the opinion that my ball crossed the wall some ten to twenty yards farther back than the spot at which he decided I should play. But even with this problematical advantage thrown in, I was still in a dilemma, for while my opponent was within reach of the hole I could not possibly carry the bunker straight, and I had to decide whether to play short, or try to carry the bunker on the left-hand side. I eventually decided on the latter alternative, and just scrambled over. My opponent had still a difficult shot to play—

a full wooden club shot—and that second shot
to the first hole at Prestwick is never an easy
one.   Misery me! he brought it off, certainly
short of the hole, but still well on the green.
Now I once again had to play two more, and
that from a most difficult position, as the ball
was not lying at all well in the rough, and,
the hole being placed very near the left-hand
edge of the green, there was very little ground
to come and go upon.   If I pitched in the rough
I might readily remain there.   If I pitched a
yard or two too far on the green I should
certainly shoot past the hole.   It was one of
those shots which spell yea or nay.   There were
no half measures possible.   Fortunately for me
the spelling was yea, and although I did not
know where the ball had finished, as the shot
was a blind one, I knew well from the spectators
that it must be very near the hole, and it was
very near, literally dead.   Yet even after this
hard labour, consequent upon that ill-fated first
shot, I was far from out of the wood, as my
opponent had still two strokes with which to

win the match.　He was miserably short, however, with his approach putt, and missed the
next one.　I still was in the land of the living,
and as he very kindly placed his tee shot in
the bunker at the next hole, I managed to sur-
vive, and once more qualify to meet Freddie
Tait.

It was only putting off the evil day, however, as once again I had to cry enough ; but
it was the one match I played against him in
which I have always considered that had fortune been just I certainly should have survived,
as Freddie played some terribly in-and-out golf ;
as usual, however, when he played against me,
his putting pulled him through.　At one period
during the round I had certainly no reason to
complain of fortune, as for some time I was
one down, and, indeed, for some holes had all my
work cut out to remain in this position.　The
fact was, however, that I should not have been
one down at all, for Tait had been extraordinarily
lucky.　For example, his tee shot to the eighth
hole was so badly topped that it actually stopped

short of the bunker in front of the tee, and yet
he eventually obtained a half in five. Again,
at the ninth hole I looked more than likely to
win the hole, as he was all over the place, but
I actually lost it. I was, in a sense, responsible for the state of affairs, as I had distinctly
failed to take advantage of the chances granted
to me.

For the next three holes I had the worst of
the play, and was lucky to arrive at the tee
to the thirteenth only one down. The next
two holes had a very serious effect on the
result of the game. At the thirteenth he was
a little unlucky in his approach, as, playing it
boldly, he ran up the hill beyond the hole and
remained there, giving him a shot which he
could not possibly lay dead. In the meanwhile
I was a little short in my approach, but hit
the back of the hole with my fourth, the ball
just failing to go down, and lying almost on
the lip of the hole. Freddie had a most difficult shot to play, as he had to borrow a lot,
and there was always a chance of the ball

still remaining in the long grass on the hill. He played it perfectly, but still the impetus which the ball gathered coming down the hill made it run some three or four yards past the hole; moreover, it looked as if he had half stymied himself. He nevertheless holed out and got a half.

After the approaches had been played to the fourteenth I again had all the best of the argument, as I was within five or six yards of the hole, and he was clean over the green some thirty to forty yards away. He put his third, however, desperately near the hole, and I proceeded to throw the hole away by first of all putting terribly short, and then missing the next one, and was consequently two down with four to play. He gave me heart of grace, however, by pulling his next tee shot to square leg, and the country on the left-hand line to that fifteenth hole at Prestwick is not at all of a rosy character. He found the ball, however, which you do not always do there. How it was lying I cannot say, but I know that he managed to put his second on the green, and he obtained a useful half. Something much the same happened at the sixteenth hole, as he once again hooked his tee shot; but number two was on the green, and another half was registered. To the seventeenth hole he varied the monotony with a bad slice from the tee. He was lying fairly well, but had a most awkward stance. Then he perpetrated an error of judgment, a sin I seldom saw him guilty of, as he took a straight-faced wooden club and tried to reach the green—with what object I can never quite make out; it was far from a certainty that I could get home in two, and being dormie, he could well afford to play short. However, he went for it, and nearly missed the ball altogether, only sending it a few yards. Then he played short, and naturally I did ditto, and eventually won the hole in five to six. His tee shot to the eighteenth was a repetition of that to the seventeenth, as it was badly sliced; but there are no hazards to the right at the last hole at Prestwick, and he was lying quite clear beside the fourteenth green. Still to me he seemed to have a most difficult approach to play, as I considered it was a most dangerous shot to try to run on account of the bank he had to cross, and if he pitched it I could not see how he was to remain near the hole. It was soon evident, however, that he knew more about the lie of the land than I did, as without any hesitation he played for the pitch and run stroke, and, greatly to my surprise, the ball ran up and over that bank with hardly a check. I still had a chance, as I was inside him with my approach, but he once and for all settled the question by laying me a dead stymie. Not that this can be said to have robbed me of the hole, as I was some six yards away and the putt was down hill, but it was a little disappointing not to be able to have a go for it.

When talking over the match afterwards I expressed surprise at the manner in which Freddie Tait played that last approach, and suggested that there must be a certain element of luck about it. I was promptly corrected by a member of the club, who remarked, "You wouldn't think so if you had seen Freddie playing a man for pennies there the other night. He brought it off nearly every time." This was an occasion when the filling in of an idle moment had been turned to good account; it was so evident when he played the shot that he was either playing it in a very haphazard manner, or else knew all about it. I could not understand where his knowledge came from, as Prestwick was not his home course, and the shot he had to play he would hardly have to play once in a dozen rounds.

The final round in that championship was a real game if ever I have seen one. To begin with, feeling ran high, as with Freddie Tait on one side and Johnnie Ball on the other, the international element was very much in evidence. Freddie was the favourite, there could be no doubt about that, but one or two English golfers had no hesitation in backing their man, and in the end a goodly portion of Scottish

"siller" crossed the border.   At one time it
looked as if it was to be the other way about,
as in the first round Scotland's hero had a
lead of five holes, most of them presented to
him by his opponent, who was putting in the
most feeble fashion; but at lunch time this
lead had been reduced to three, and the difference between three and five holes is a very
material one.   In the afternoon there was a
very different tale to tell, as this lead of three
quickly disappeared, and there was a ding-dong
struggle.   Freddie was driving wildly, one of
his feats being to hook his tee shot to the
twelfth hole clean over the burn.   It was quite
a prodigious feat in the art of hooking, and
many of the spectators who were close to the
burn had no idea where the ball had gone, and
could not understand why he was dropping
another; they could not realise that it had
travelled clean over their heads.   Eventually
Johnnie Ball stood one up with two to play,
and then a hole was played which will always
remain as a landmark in the history of the game.

To begin the story, the bunker which guarded the seventeenth green was more than half full of water. Freddie Tait put his second right into the middle of the water. Johnnie Ball played a shot which, personally, I thought was over, but the ominous signal was given, " down." When the players arrived on the scene, Freddie Tait's ball was floating, but not floating too well, as it was certainly not quite on the surface of the water, whilst his opponent's was on the hard sand, between the water and the sleepers. Freddie walked into that water, which may have been anything between nine to fifteen inches in depth; as one Scottish journal remarked, "Tait walked in as a soldier should." Whether it referred to Freddie's bearing or to his bravery I have never been able to understand, as from the latter point of view it would seem almost worth while getting your feet wet to save a championship; but he went in and rightly too, for if he had lifted the ball and paid the penalty he would have been in a hopeless position. The shot out could barely have been improved upon:

L

he ploughed it out on to the green, and oh, the wild shouts that arose! I shall never forget them. In the meanwhile Johnnie Ball had, in my opinion, quite as difficult, if not a more difficult, stroke to play. He was near the sleepers, and those sleepers are very upright, and the sand on which his ball lay was as hard as adamant. The latter was the difficulty he had to surmount, as it is far from easy to raise a ball quickly from a hard surface; but he did surmount it, as very few men could have done. I do not think that many appreciated what a difficult shot it was, and I have always thought that it has never been quite given its correct value as a wonderful recovery. Eventually that hole was halved, and England stood dormie one, only to lose the last hole, where Freddie holed an excellent three to save himself. Then came another sensational hole. Both drives were good, straight, and far. Freddie had to play the odd, and an excellent shot it was, never off the pin. I was standing on the hill to the left of the hole

when the ball pitched, and I have always considered that it was not at all well treated, as it
seemed to get a shooting fall, the ground just
short of the hole being very hummocky.   In
any case, whether it was owing to the way in
which the stroke was played, or to the unfortunate fall, the fact remains that it left the
striker a putt of some seven to ten yards.
Johnnie Ball's approach was also *ruled* on the
pin.   What would it do? skid over the green
like the other, or pull up?   We were not long
in doubt, as from the very first bounce it was
evident that it was not going to travel far, and
it gently trickled on until it passed the hole
by about seven feet.   Freddie Tait had a most
difficult putt.   He made a good bid, but it
never looked like going in, and everything depended upon Johnnie Ball's seven-footer.   A
man standing beside me remarked, "These are
just the ones he misses."   I thought to myself,
"No, these are just the ones he holes."   Had
it been three or four feet I should have been
more anxious,   From where we stood we could

not see the outline of the hole, and it was impossible to tell whether the ball was going in or not, but I liked the look of the striker as the ball was travelling. I knew his attitudes well, and was not at all surprised when the ball disappeared. I have seen some excitement at championship meetings, but never anything quite equal to that at Prestwick in 1899.

The Open Championship that year at Sandwich was a very uninteresting event. Harry Vardon was to blame, as his extraordinary run of successes since his win at Prestwick in the previous year had made the event appear almost a certainty for him, and a certainty he made it, for he led from start to finish ; in racing phraseology, he won "pulling up." Certainly Jack White eventually finished within five strokes of him, but Harry had a lot in hand when the last round came to be played. Many who saw him play that round expressed the opinion that if he had still had the other rounds to play he would have won by more than five strokes. This, however, is a somewhat natural assumption when a player can afford to play his last round steadily and take no undue risks. In those days, however, Harry Vardon hardly ever broke down, even in a minor degree. I chiefly remember that championship owing to there being at one time a grave doubt as to whether I should succeed in qualifying for the second day's play; failure to do so would then have been a very humiliating affair. In the first round I was ten strokes behind Vardon, but in the second round I was doing much better, as I holed out the first ten holes in 43, and in consequence felt very confident of being included in the select. I received rather a rude shock, however, when a friend came up and remarked, " How are you doing ? " " Oh, much better," I said ; " I am here in 43." " How many strokes were you behind Vardon this morning ? " I replied, " Ten." " Let me see," he said. " You will have to hurry up if you want to play to-morrow ; you have still two strokes to play with. If Vardon takes more than two strokes from you in the next eight holes you can put your clubs by for the rest of the meeting. He has holed these ten holes out in 36." I suggested that he was drawing the long-bow. " It is absolutely true," was the reply. Fortunately Harry was merciful, and did a little bit of a break-down in those eight holes.

CHAPTER VIII

Naturally I shall always remember the year
1900, as it was a year in which I at last satisfied
an ambition which had been deep rooted in my
soul for a very long time. The title of amateur
champion was a very long time coming my way;
I had struggled for it for twelve years, and in
each succeeding year it seemed to be going
farther and farther away from me. I cannot
say, even after the many failures that had been
my lot, that I had yet arrived at a state of
despair. Still I knew well that every year I
approached the competition with a gradually
increasing feeling of anxiety, and I was beginning
to realise that it would have been well had fate
been a little more kind to me in 1891, when
Laidlay beat me at the twentieth hole. At the
time I didn't think much of the occurrence, as

I had the naturally optimistic feeling inseparable from youth that my time was sure to come. It did come at last, but its coming was just a little belated: nearly nine years had passed by, and I was arriving at an age when my game could hardly be expected to improve. In this Amateur Championship, played at Sandwich, there were two notable faces missing, viz., Freddie Tait and Johnnie Ball. The former, alas! was no more, and the latter still at the front in South Africa. This made my task much more simple than it would have been, as these two undoubtedly stand out as the two best match players in the history of the championship.

Before the championship the usual preliminary event at Sandwich took place, the contest for the St. George's Vase, and this Robert Maxwell won easily. All who saw him play expressed the same opinion, and that was, that he was playing a magnificent long game. Personally I made the most awful start imaginable in this event through sheer nervousness, as for the first few holes I could not hit the ball when near the hole; on the very first green I took four to hole out, and, moreover, was never up to the hole until the ball went in, a very bad sign indeed, as I knew well.   My start panned out as follows: 6, 5, 5, 7, 5; but eventually I reached the turn in 45.   After that I pulled myself together and came home in 38, and in the afternoon finished in 78.   But I did not like that nervous start, and was not at all happy about it, as a repetition of such an occurrence would, for a certainty, cause me to say good-bye to championship honours at a very early date.   The danger was all the greater as, all being well, I had to meet Maxwell on the second day.   This meeting came off in due course, and I candidly acknowledge that I started feeling very nervous.   I had heard that he was driving very well, and had a practical confirmation of this rumour at the very first hole. I hit a fair ball, but I found myself sixty or seventy yards behind, and, although this did not happen often, I generally found myself having to play the odd from some considerable distance behind.

However, I knew Sandwich well enough to realise that, notwithstanding what some critics say,
long driving is not everything there.   Accuracy
tells there as much, if not more, than on any
of the championship courses.   I was one down
at the third, but I won the fourth and also the
fifth, and then came a very crucial incident.
It was at the " Maiden " hole: I had the
best of the tee shot, and had nearly holed out
in two.   Maxwell had a comparatively easy
putt for a half, but missed it.   Still he did
the next best thing to holing it, as he laid
me a dead stymie, his ball being only an inch
or so from the hole.   Now, the green at this
" Maiden " hole at Sandwich is almost an ideal
one on which to attempt to loft stymies, as it
has plenty of grass on it, and it is consequently
very easy to get under the ball; under ordinary conditions, I should have had no hesitation in going for the stroke, but this was
a championship, and had I knocked him in,
as I certainly would have done had I hit his
ball, I should have lost a hole which I had

every right to win. In addition to the actual
loss of the hole there was also the moral effect
to take into account, as although the match
was still in its comparative infancy, it was
certainly at a critical stage. I eventually went
for the shot, and luckily brought it off, making
me two up. The seventh hole was another
hole full of incident. I hit what I considered
a really good tee shot, but my opponent hit a
better. When we arrived over the bunker a
ball was to be seen perched on the plateau.
I knew that was mine, but I could not see his
anywhere. Eventually I discerned it away in
the distance, down in the strath. I felt inclined
to ask the spectators if any one had helped it
along by throwing it. From my position I
could not carry the bunker, so I played round
on the left-hand side, and had the luck to
run past the left-hand edge of the hazard. He
was easily on with an iron, but a little wide
on the right. Still I was more than twice as
far from the hole as he was. I ran my third
up about ten feet from the hole, and he over-

ran his about six or seven feet. A good deal depended upon those putts, and I was more than thankful to see mine go down, and the feeling of thankfulness was greatly added to when his did not. From that point I never looked back. I played with confidence, which meant everything, and I won on the fifteenth green. I have heard people when discussing that match remark that there was only one in it. There may have been only one in it at the fifteenth hole, but in the earlier stages there was more than one in it by a long way. Those two incidents at the sixth and seventh holes had a very great effect upon the result.

From the very start I had looked upon Robert Maxwell as *the* great stumbling-block to overcome. There were naturally others who had to be treated with very great respect; but the St. George's Vase result, and moreover the tales told as to how it was accomplished, impressed upon me that he was playing the species of game which is only begotten of confidence, and, not at all liking that class of man, I was consequently very pleased to see him *hors de combat*. Once I was past him the task of reaching the semi-final stage was not an overwhelmingly difficult one, and in saying this I trust that the two men I defeated will not think me discourteous or lacking in appreciation of their merits; but the fact remains that I happened to win both rounds in a very easy manner. Then I had to meet John Graham, jun.; he was then not quite the player he is now, and, moreover, had not the experience he can now claim. The start to that round almost bordered on the ludicrous. The first hole had to be played against a slight head-wind, and it wanted two real good ones to get home. My opponent slightly sliced his tee shot, and with his second had to play short on the right. I was well placed with my tee shot, and had a go for it. I knew well that it was just as much as I could do, but I just brought it off, and as the ball was never off the pin, and only just cleared the hazard guarding the green, there seemed every possibility that it must be very near the hole. Graham carefully played his third, and it was very evident where it was; but when we came up only one ball was to be seen on the green, and that was not mine. I couldn't make it out, and was looking about in bewilderment when a reporter some fifty yards away called out something. I could not exactly catch what he said, but one of the spectators did, as he remarked, "He says it is in the hole," and sure enough it was. I don't know whether this untoward accident had any detrimental effect on the play of my opponent, but he did not play at all well, and the match was over on the thirteenth green.

This early finish enabled me to witness the conclusion of the other penultimate tie, that between James Robb and Bramston. The latter had been very much fancied from the start, and justifiably fancied, as a few weeks previously he had put up a performance at Westward Ho which was worthy of any amateur living. It was on the occasion of the Easter meeting of the Royal North Devon Club, and it so happened that at this meeting the Royal Liverpool Club had sent a team down, and a team of the Oxford and Cambridge Society were also there. Johnnie Bramston at that time was only about nineteen years of age; in consequence his experience must have been very limited, and experience is always presumed to be a great factor in serious match play. Now it so happened that the powers that be in the Society had a certain degree of difficulty in arranging the order in which their team should play. This must always be the case with a team which is collected from literally all parts of the globe.

On this occasion the difficulty was a little more pronounced than usual, so that it was decided to play the matches in a kind of "anyhow" order, and at the same time give the youngsters a chance, with the result that Bramston was placed to play second to Humphrey Ellis. On a mere question of reputation he possibly had no right to be placed in that exalted position, but he quickly proved that on form he

might with good reason have been given the
absolute place of honour, as he began by
trouncing Horace Hutchinson to the extent
of ten holes, and that in one single round : he
followed this up by beating me by three holes,
and in doing so thoroughly deserved his win.
In the second match he backed up this form
by beating John Low by five holes, and wound
up the week by defeating Humphrey Ellis, four
very respectable scalps to hang at his girdle.
When he arrived at Sandwich there were evident
signs that he had not by any means lost his
form, as he tied for second place in the St.
George's Vase. In the championship he went
on his way rejoicing until he reached the penultimate round, and there can be no doubt
that the majority anticipated that he would
even proceed farther, notwithstanding Robb's
reputation as a match player. Being otherwise employed, I did not see anything of the
early part of the game, but I was told that
Robb, though outplayed with the wooden clubs,
was saving himself by his short game. As one

man remarked to me when I joined the crowd going to the fifteenth hole, "Robb is outplayed, but he is putting beautifully; he has just holed a picture at the last hole, after having all the worst of it." Whether these repeated recoveries on the part of the Scotsman had by degrees had an effect upon the temperament of his opponent is a question which could only be settled by the latter himself, but I have seldom seen a man break down in a more complete fashion than Bramston did that afternoon at Sandwich. The trouble commenced with his pitch to the fifteenth green, which he hit all along the ground right into the bunker. Robb played anything but a good approach and might readily have taken six to the hole, but Bramston did not seem to trouble about this; he simply walked into the bunker and hacked away at the ball with the same club he had played his approach with. This left him one down. His tee shot to the sixteenth was very like his approach to the previous hole, as it was also topped, and finished in the water

M

hazard. He picked it out, dropped it, and did not seem to care in the slightest where his next shot went. Robb also won that hole. The seventeenth saw the finish, as Bramston presented his enemy with the match by completely missing his approach. Never in my life have I seen such a complete break-down. It seemed impossible to believe that a man who had been playing with such sublime confidence could go to pieces so utterly. He himself very aptly summed up the situation when he remarked, "It was not a question of nerves; it was absolute paralysis." And it certainly appeared very akin to that disease.

I have often been asked the question, "Whom would you rather have met—Robb or Bramston?" Before the final round took place it was a very difficult query to answer, but after the final was over it was infinitely more simple to give a reply. There can be no doubt, however, that just at that time Johnnie Bramston was playing a very strong game, and, had his boyish confidence not deserted him, would

have been a very difficult man to beat, as he
was hitting a very long ball. In fact, right
through the meeting he was playing a very
fine game with his wooden clubs, and I certainly should not have had an advantage over
him in this department of the game, while I
must acknowledge that I anticipated having at
least a little bit the best of the wooden club
play against Robb. The only thing I was afraid
of was his putting, for which I had the most
wholesome respect. Few men strike the ball
more freely on a putting green than James Robb,
and what is more, he always looks as if he was
going to hole the ball. As it happened he was
not particularly successful with his putter; not
that he did not putt well, but they would not
go in for him, and in the first round I certainly had none the worst of it on the greens,
for which I was truly thankful. And in finishing three up at lunch-time I was decidedly
fortunate, as a halved round would have been
a truer reflex of the run of the play.

In the afternoon my opponent's driving broke

down.   Whether he was pressing or not is
not for me to say, but the result appeared
to suggest that such was the case.   He was
distinctly hurrying his swing, with disastrous
results, and in consequence my task was not a
difficult one.   I was nine up before the turn
was reached, and eventually won on the eleventh
green.

The Open Championship that year was played
at St. Andrews, a green which, I candidly acknowledge, completely beats me, at least when
I have to play by the rule of card and pencil.
I have been told by kind friends that this only
proves what an excellent test of the game it is.
This may or may not be, but there is certainly
something about the course which is not in
keeping with my temperament; I have a rooted
dislike to hitting a ball right down the middle
of the course and finding it trapped.

Talking with some men before the championship, I happened to remark that it was somewhat curious that I was hardly ever drawn with
a really good player.   One of them remarked,

" Well, you have got one this time; you are drawn with Harry Vardon." Not knowing that the draw had taken place, I took his remark as a mere joke. He was quite correct, as I afterwards found out.

That there was going to be a big crowd was very evident, and a St. Andrews crowd requires a deal of managing; great then was my surprise to hear, on the day before the championship commenced, a rumour that the executive had decided not to use ropes. I could not believe it, but on my interviewing one of the committee he confirmed this rumour. The explanation given for this extraordinary decision was, that the committee had come to the conclusion that they could not possibly supply men with ropes for one individual couple in a *scoring* competition, as it would not be fair to the remainder of the competitors. There may on a close analysis be found a suspicion of logic in this argument; but, considering that it was almost a foregone conclusion that fully 75 per cent. of the gallery would follow Vardon and myself, it could hardly be said that we could be gaining any material advantage from their presence, even with the aid of ropes.

As I anticipated, this decision made our game a comparative fiasco, as, whilst the gallery were fairly calm and collected. for the first few holes, they then suddenly exhibited a decided inclination to obtain seats right in front of the house; if they couldn't obtain stalls they wanted the nearest seat to them. The efforts of the men decorated with rosettes to keep them in order were quite futile. The children led the way, then came the women, and the men naturally followed in their wake. Result—an absolute stampede after the tee shots were played, and one never got near one's ball without cleaving a way through a solid mass of humanity. You can stand that kind of thing for a certain period, but it requires a man with a very equable temperament to put up with it for two rounds in one day; that year at St. Andrews I must say I found the man so blessed, and it was Harry Vardon. He never once exhibited the slightest sign of irritation, though he really would have been justified had he done so.

Trying as the crowd was in the morning round, it was as nothing to that which had to be encountered in the afternoon. In the first place, the numbers had been considerably augmented; in the second place, those who had followed round in the morning had learnt a valuable lesson from their previous experience, which was, that if you did not hurry you were left—and they did not fail to hurry that after-noon. Going to the tenth hole it almost ap-proached the ludicrous. The tee was placed well on the left-hand side, and as there was a wind blowing from the right, it was necessary to play well out in that direction in order to keep clear of the rough on the left. The crowd lined up quite close in, with the result that it was impossible to play in the desired direction without there being a very grave chance of disturbing somebody's features. We waited some moments in the hope that some one would appreciate the difficulties under which we were labouring, and eventually an elderly gentleman with a rosette in his coat kindly asked us if he could do anything. I tried my best to explain the difficulty, which he realised, and he valiantly tried to put matters right. His intentions were no doubt excellent, and, moreover, he was extremely thorough in his methods, as he started at the beginning of the long line of spectators and politely requested them *individually* to keep back a little, as the competitors could not possibly play. They very amicably responded, but only individually, and no sooner had he proceeded some distance along the line than those whom he had first requested promptly moved back to their original position. They were just like a herd of sheep, and eventually, seeing the case was hopeless, we both had to drive into the rough on the left-hand side of the course.

Going to the fifteenth hole I had a rather amusing experience. I pulled my tee shot right through the middle of the running crowd, and no doubt many of them played involuntary football with it.   Harry Vardon hit his down the middle of the course.   The crowd immediately lined up behind his ball, leaving me a solid phalanx of spectators to play over.   The position was absolutely hopeless.   I couldn't possibly play: there did not seem to be any one who would take on him the responsibility of informing the crowd of the situation, and I certainly did not feel equal to it myself.   I had done enough work of that description for one day, so I calmly sat down beside my ball and awaited developments.   The fact was, *I was lost!*   Eventually I was found, and after a judicious herding of the crowd the game was allowed to proceed.

This species of amusement went on all the way round.   Going to the sixteenth we were not allowed to play to the left of the " Principal's Nose," we had to play straight between that hazard and the railway.   Going to the seventeenth Harry Vardon wished to play his tee shot away to the left.   He pathetically

remarked, " I cannot do it without cutting some
one's nose off. I shall have to play out for a
pull." And a pull he got, as he pulled clean
over the heads of the crowd into the whins
on the left, and very few of them even noticed
it, with the result that there was another delay.
I shall never forget Harry Vardon that day.
He stood it all like a saint. He seemed infinitely more amused than angry; it must have
cost him a stroke or two, although perhaps
hardly the championship, as Taylor eventually
won easily, finishing with a sensational 75, and
finishing, it may be said, in front of a crowd
who were kept in their proper place by the aid
of a rope and many stalwarts to look after it.
The executive had learnt a lesson. My own
participation in that championship consisted of
one meteoric flash, the first ten holes in round
number one, for which the total was 39. The
remaining eight holes for that round cost me 44.

CHAPTER IX

WHEN I travelled up to St. Andrews in 1901 I cannot say that I was feeling exactly full of confidence, as I knew that I was not playing quite as consistently as I had been in the previous year, and there were other reasons also. First, the field is invariably a strong one on the classic green, as there is an introduction of local talent, which is always a serious difficulty for any one to overcome. Not that this St. Andrews local element ever win championships on their own green—they in truth seem to do better when away from the inspiring influence of their traditional home—but whether they win or not, they are invariably desperately difficult men to defeat. They certainly add to the difficulties of the man who eventually gets through by clearing out the weak. The result is that you have to meet a strong man literally every round, and the stronger the man you have to meet naturally the greater the possibility of defeat in the individual round.   Again, I cannot say that I fancied myself as even a match-player over the classic green, and this notwithstanding that I had once very nearly won a championship there, for since that time, I always found it very difficult to restrain a certain feeling of irritation from overcoming me when I drove into any of the bunkers from the tee.   This time, however, I made up my mind that, come what might, I would play the game in an equable frame of mind.   If I did get into bunkers I would just play out, and treat these disasters as necessary evils.   I may say, however, that I had in addition made out a plan of campaign to avoid these bunkers as much as possible, for I had come to the conclusion that it was the man who steered clear of them who eventually succeeded in winning over St. Andrews.   This was a little mental programme which sounds very well in theory, and before the event seems very easy to carry out, but it is not nearly so easy to stick to in the heat of the battle. Still, on the whole, my temperament remained very much what I intended right through the week's play; though I may have on occasions felt a little irritable, it was only momentarily, and I quickly pulled myself together. As regards the avoiding of the hazards, I remained most faithful to that principle, for wherever there was any grave risk of trouble from the tee I invariably took a short club, with which I knew I could keep fairly straight. As an example, not once did I use my driver going to the sixth hole, and I have not the slightest doubt that this restraint paid me in the long run.

I won my first few heats fairly easily, and I looked like doing the same even when I met Laidlay, who played such a nervous, halting game on the outward half that at one time I stood five up. Then, however, he began to improve and I began to go back, till I found myself scratching for halves, some of which I did not succeed in obtaining. The result was that I only found myself two up with three to play. Again I had quite the worst of the approach to the sixteenth hole, as I had a long putt to lay dead, and he had one which he might readily have holed. I fortunately managed to get mine dead, and he putted very short, missed his next, and the match was over. Had the putting gone the other way I should have only been one up with two to play, not at all pleasant after being at one time five up. Indeed, on the sixteenth green I didn't at all like the situation. In my next round I only played seven holes when my opponent had to retire, and heat number five I won some way from home. This brought me to the semi-final, and against Horace Hutchinson, curiously enough the only time I had ever met him in a championship. It was a peculiar game. He first of all presented me with a lead of three holes; then the boot was on the other leg, and I found myself one down with five to play. At this point I witnessed, with more than an average degree of satisfaction, a well-hit tee shot of his pitch plump into the middle of the " Beardies " and never come out. I gave them a very wide berth, taking a short club for safety, and was rewarded by winning the hole. This disaster appeared to have an effect on my opponent's play, as he played the fifteenth and sixteenth indifferently, and I annexed them both and became dormie. Up to that time I had never been called upon to play the seventeenth hole, but I had already made up my mind how I was going to play it, and that was right away to the left, keeping my second shot on the line of the first green. It is a peculiar line maybe, but I infinitely prefer to play the third shot straight at the pot bunker in place of trying to slip past it from the right-hand side. Indeed, whenever I saw Andrew Kirkaldy play the hole he invariably played that line, or at least whenever he could not get near the edge of the green with his second, and Andrew's knowledge of St. Andrews is sufficiently good for me to follow. Eventually I played a shot which might have ended in disaster. There was certainly a risk in playing it as boldly as I did, but I was in no mood for half measures at that seventeenth hole, as I had seen it frittered away too often by half-hearted safety play.

I played my third straight at the left-hand corner of the bunker with a wooden spoon, trying at the same time to put as much cut on the ball as possible.   Fortunately for me I got that cut on, for although the ball pitched on the green, it pulled up so quickly that it stopped some feet short of the road, and I had no difficulty in obtaining the requisite half.   I have heard different opinions expressed about that shot, some saying it was one of the best shots they had ever seen played, and although I played it myself I cannot help thinking that it had its merits.   On the other hand, one or two severe critics said that it was a silly shot, which deserved to be punished, and that it was not golf.   Perhaps it was not quite the traditional way to approach that much revered hole.   It was a stroke which savoured of want of respect for the hole's many difficulties, but I like these silly disrespectful shots, they seem to pay in championships.

The other semi-final, between John Low and John Graham, jun., was a very close affair.   The former stood three up with four to play, but lost

the succeeding three holes, and the odds seemed
to be on the Royal Liverpool player, the last
hole at St. Andrews being essentially the hole
for a long driver.   As it happened, however,
John Low played it perfectly, and John Graham,
jun., did not; he missed his second shot, and
this cost him the hole and the match.   I shall
always remember that match on account of one
incident which occurred when the last hole was
being played.   I had gone to the top balcony of
the club to see the finish, and without knowing
exactly how the match stood; but I had heard
that Low was three up and four to play, and
when I saw his opponent drive off to the last
hole it was evident that the match was still
alive.   Then a press messenger came running
up, and intimated that the players were all
square.   In the room behind me there was a
table, around which were grouped four men
deep in the intricacies of bridge, one of whom
I noticed had apparently something to do with
the management of the meeting—at least he
sported the badge of a club official.   I was

N

casually asked how the games were going. I
replied, "There is a good match coming up.
Graham has been three down with four to play
against Low, but they are now all square with
one to play." I rather anticipated that there
would be a stampede to see the finish from
the balcony, from which coign of vantage you
can see every shot played. But not a bit of
it! The four *golfers* proceeded once again
to deal the cards, and he who sported the
official badge remarked, "I don't take much
interest in it now; all my horses are knocked
out," apparently referring to the sweepstakes.
I said nothing but thought a lot.

I must candidly acknowledge that I thought
I should beat my old friend John Low in that
final round, even although it had to be played
at St. Andrews, over which green he is, no
doubt, a more dangerous opponent than on any
other course in the kingdom. Over eighteen
holes I should have been anxious, but over
thirty-six holes I had every confidence. The
fact was, I had not a very high opinion of his

wooden club play, as I had never seen him
play them really well; admitting that his head-
work and intimate knowledge of the green,
backed up by his putting, might mitigate in
a degree deficiencies from the tee and through
the green, I still had an idea that his wooden
club play was sure to find him out in a thirty-
six hole contest. It did not however; he
played those wooden clubs of his as I had
never seen him play them before. I kept waiting for the serious mistakes, and they did
not come. In the first round I was distinctly
fortunate in being able to hold on to him for
the first twelve holes; indeed, if the truth is to
be told, it was only by the aid of superior putting that I managed to do so. Towards the
end of the round I managed at last to get a
little the best of the long play, and taking advantage of the opportunity, finished with a three-
hole advantage; but I cannot say that I quite
deserved this lead, and felt that I had no reason
to cavil at fortune.

In the second round I began by winning

the first hole; at the fifth I added another
to my lead, and stood five up. This appeared
very comfortable; but I had to reckon with a
man who always tries to the very last stroke,
and he gradually began to get those five holes
back. Still keeping up his accurate wooden club
play, he suddenly found his putting shoes. His
first real long one, however, was at the thirteenth, where he holed out from the far dim
distance; as I was not dead after playing the
odd it probably made no difference, but it
tickled the crowd immensely, and that was
something. Eventually I stood one up with
four to play. The fifteenth was a peculiarly
played hole and full of incident. I had all
the best of the first two shots, and was quite
close to the green. He was very short with his
second, and for his approach decided to play
a species of patent spared shot with a wooden
club. The crowd were cleared away from the
left-hand side of the course, and it was evident
that he intended to slice the shot into the wind.
He didn't fail to slice it by any means, as the

ball finished in the rough on the right, short of the green. In the meanwhile I had placed my approach past the hole. Playing the odd, he pitched the ball up about six yards from the hole. Now I had to play the like from a distance of about eight yards. It was not an easy putt. It was down hill, and there was a borrow from the right, and to remain dead I had to just crawl over a sharp hill, which was situated about six feet from the hole. Difficult as the putt was, a portion of the crowd, who stood within about six feet of my ball, made it none the easier by keeping up a running commentary as to the possibilities of the ball not going dead. I made a request that they might not talk whilst I was playing, but they paid but little attention to this request, and finally I had to play, conversation or no conversation. From the time the ball left the club it appeared on the short side, and my friends behind did not fail to realise the fact, as they addressed the ball in all sorts of terms, many of which would barely stand reproduction, and truly fervent were the expressions when the ball just failed to surmount the hill, and remained some five or six feet short. As one sportsman audibly remarked, "The —— winna hole it,—you'll see." I may say I was rather of his opinion; but the audible endorsement of my thoughts seemed somewhat unnecessary. Then Master John Low proceeded to putt and made no mistake whatever, as the ball went in and never looked like going anywhere else. Then the cheering commenced in no half-hearted fashion, but I did not mind that: it was only natural, as the effort was a great one. I did get my putt down, but it was a lucky one, only just scraping in. The only noise *I* heard was the remark of Johnnie Low, "Well putted, Harold," and that compensated for much; but, in truth, it was far from a good putt, as I mistook the line altogether, and no one was more surprised than I when the ball fell into the hole.

Still one up with three to go. The sixteenth was not at all well played by either, and eventually I was left with a putt of about three feet for a half in five. My effort was a very weak one, and many of the followers of the game very quickly appreciated the fact, as there was a wild shout of exultation, perhaps quite excusable under the circumstances. I was wandering to the next tee feeling in a semi-dejected, irritable frame of mind, possibly the worst state a man playing a serious game of golf can drift into, when an excited spectator, caring little and heeding less, made a bee line for a front place, and in his mad career charged full into me; he nearly knocked me over, and as he travelled by on his hurricane passage I could not help hearing the remark: "We'll teach these b——y Englishmen." This freely expressed opinion had a most salutary effect upon me: a modified form of anger took the place of the nervous hesitation which pervaded my system, and I said to myself, "Will you?" It was just the necessary antidote I required, and I began to play those last two holes as if they were the only two holes to be played in the championship. I forgot all about the fact that at one time I stood five up, and was now all even ; it was a new game, and I played it as such.

I cannot quite remember what my opponent did with his first and second shot at that hole. I simply concentrated my attention on my own strokes. I remember, however, that he was well short of the green in three, and had quite a difficult approach to play for his fourth. In the meanwhile I had taken the line which I considered best — that is, well to the left ; but I had slightly hooked my second, and was farther away from the green than I cared for. As in the previous round, I decided to chance the bunker. I asked my caddie, David Herd, whether I could reach the road, and he expressed an opinion that he would be surprised if I did. This was quite enough for me, as I had learnt by this time that he knew the distances at St. Andrews more than well, and in consequence I took my driver and played a full shot—a shot which eventually finished within a few yards of the hole. As in the previous round, there was a decided risk in playing this shot; but a half-hearted shot might have ended in losing the hole, and I had the opinion of my caddie that it was very improbable that I should get as far as the road. I have heard people express the opinion that it was the finest shot that they have ever seen played in a championship. With this I cannot agree, as to me there seemed only one risk, and that was the possibility of getting into the pot bunker guarding the green, and that was a difficult object to hit from a distance of about 190 yards. If I had just struck it I might readily have lost the hole; but my opponent was so far from the green with his third that there was still more than a good chance of a half, as he could barely expect to hole out in anything less than six. As it so happened, he put himself out of court by placing his approach in the road, and eventually gave up the hole; but the proximity of my ball to the hole undoubtedly made him play a bold shot, as nothing over five

could have been of any use to him, and it was
in rightly playing the bold game that he came
to grief. Dormie one. The last hole could be
nicely reached in two, but both shots had to
be hit. From the tee I had slightly the worst
of the argument, as I was too much on the
left-hand side of the course, and when I came
up I found that I was lying in a divot mark,
of which there are more than a good many on
this part of the links. Still there was nothing
to carry and that meant much; so I took my
driver in the hope that I could "spring" the
ball out and get a long run upon it. Once
again the shot came off. The ball possibly
did not carry more than 120 yards; but I
knew well from the strain on the shaft that
it had plenty of steam behind it, and that
once it landed, it would run like a hare: my
surmise was not wrong, as it mounted the hill
short of the green without a falter, and toddled
on until old Tom, who held the flag, had to
step aside to let it pass. Not a sound came
forth from the crowd, their powers of articula-

tion seemed suddenly to have deserted them, but from the spectators lining up behind the green came one very decided sign of appreciation. It was a Zulu war whoop, a sound which I had heard before, and it came from a good strong pair of lungs, and, moreover, it was meant. A man close beside me remarked, "Good heavens, what is that?" I simply replied, "I know," and I did. This shot literally settled the verdict; Johnnie Low made quite a good bid for a three, but even had he done it I should still have been left with an easy putt to win the match: as it was, a four was quite sufficient.

The Open Championship was that year played at Muirfield, a green on which people consider I ought of necessity to do well, simply for the reason that I happened to win on the first occasion the championship was played there. Now I have no strong predilection for the Muirfield course, but that is another story. I did, however, realise that year that it is necessary to drive comparatively straight at Muirfield. In the

very first round of the championship I sliced
more than one tee shot, and these shots met
with due punishment, with the result that I took
89 for the first round.

I have only one grievance in that round, and
that was, that a really good approach to the
fifteenth hit the top of the sleepers and bounded
back ·into a truly horrible place, with the consequence that an eight was placed on my card,
and I did not play too carefully for the remaining five holes; but well as I played in the
following rounds, it cannot be said that it made
any difference to the championship, as Braid,
Vardon, and Taylor would still have been in
front of me; again it must be considered that
when doing so well on the second day, I was
playing without that feeling of responsibility
which is inseparable from a contest in which
you have a decided chance of success. This was
the year in which Braid won his first championship. A brilliant round of 74 at his third
attempt placed him in a comparatively safe
position, and I am told that he might have

done better in his last effort, which totalled 80, had he not played on the safe side. There was quite a dramatic finish to this final round. To the last hole he hit a very long ball from the tee, and was within easy reach of the green. I was one of a group of spectators standing behind the green. It was evident that Braid was using an iron club. He hit at it desperately hard, and there was a smothered groan when a bright object was seen to be flying along the ground. There was a general impression that he had almost missed the ball, but suddenly there was a cry, "Look out!" and the ball came down flop on to the green, and finished up on the teeing ground to the first hole, which was placed almost directly behind the last green. The object we had seen careering along the turf was the head of the club, which had broken off short at the socket. Harry Vardon had eventually a chance of tieing with Braid, as an aggregate of twelve for the last three holes would have given him the same total. Everything depended upon his approach to the sixteenth hole.   He took the trouble to have a good look at it, and then quietly dropped the ball into the bunker, a species of sin Harry is very seldom guilty of.   This settled his chance once and for all.

CHAPTER X

If I approached the championship of 1901 at St. Andrews in a certain spirit of what might be termed waning confidence, it was as nothing to the feelings which had possession of me when the Amateur Championship, in the ordinary cycle of events, had to be played at Hoylake in 1902. I simply had no faith in my game. The rhythm of my swing was all away, and I could not time the ball at all. I knew it before I ever travelled to the championship. There was just the possible hope that I might strike a happy vein of play during the championship week, but such hopes proved vain, as from the international match onwards I played very scratchy golf, hardly playing a single stroke with even the slightest degree of confidence. Fortune was kind to me in this respect, that I had the most simple positions in the draw it was possible to imagine, for in the first four rounds I had not to meet a single player who in ordinary club events could be classed better than scratch. ·I scraped through those four rounds, but in one of them, against a clubmate, A. C. Blain, I had every reason to be thankful, as he had quite the best of the final holes played, and I should have met a well-merited fate had I been beaten. The game lasted until the twenty - first hole, and that one I certainly should have lost, as with my third I was tucked up under the bank of the bunker guarding the green, and should almost to a certainty have taken seven to hole out. He appeared to have the hole at his mercy, but fate was kind to me, in that he missed two consecutive approach shots, and finally gave up the hole. Sooner or later I must come across a player who could play sufficiently well to beat me, and I knew that my life was not going to be a long one. The end came in the fifth round, when I had to meet Sidney Fry. All he had to do was to play steadily, and he did it, with the result that he won on the sixteenth green. I may say, however, that his run and pitch shots with his jigger were mainly instrumental in pulling him through, as time after time he placed these shots within a yard or so of the hole, and then invariably holed out. But this is barely a cause for complaint, as it is a habit which Sidney Fry has.

In the penultimate round my conqueror had to meet Robert Maxwell, who, from the very start of the tournament, was probably the most favoured one in the eyes of the public, and, now that the number had been reduced to a mere matter of four players, was a very warm favourite. It was a game in which neither player can be said to have done himself justice, as many indifferent strokes were played; but Maxwell's defeat was mainly due to the missing of two very short putts. The first of these failures happened at the second hole, when he had quite a short one for the half, but never hit the ball hard enough; the other occurred on the seventeenth green, when he

o

again missed one which appeared to the spectators to be more easily measured by inches than feet, though no doubt it was longer than it looked. It was a very crucial hole to lose in more ways than one, for first, from the practical point of view, it left him one down with one to play. Secondly, it was a hole which he appeared much more likely to win than to lose; his opponent had half missed his second, and it was only by the aid of that deadly run up of his with his jigger that Fry was enabled to make a bid for a four. These little turns of fortune's wheel are apt to have a little moral effect on the play for the following hole.

The other semi-final round between Robb and Hutchings was a curious affair; Robb had the most extraordinary luck at the eleventh hole, where, after slicing his drive far to the right, he holed out with his iron; Hutchings, who was at that time one down and looked like squaring the match, being close to the hole with his tee shot, was simply left with the possibility of a half, which he failed to obtain. Great as was Robb's luck at this hole, he had no reason to be beholden to fortune at the next, as a beautifully played approach trickled past the hole into the pond beyond. I have heard this particular shot stigmatised as an ill-advised one; but I believe the truth is that he used a club which he had borrowed, and was not quite aware of its power. I cannot help thinking that that pond beyond the twelfth hole at Hoylake is hardly a fair hazard; at least, the extreme penalty of dropping behind and losing a stroke is a little severe on the player who plays boldly for the pin. Robb's stroke on this particular occasion was a really good one, and deserved a better fate. Eventually Hutchings stood one up with two to play, and he had no difficulty in winning on the seventeenth green, as Robb played that hole just about as badly as I have ever seen a hole played. He began by hooking his drive right into the bunker guarding the out-of-bounds field on the left — a feat not very often accomplished. His recovery was far from a good one, and his third was even worse, as he almost missed it altogether. It represented a real solid break-down.

When the championship week began there were a certain number of the entrants who were armed with the American rubber-cored ball; in fact, it is more than probable that every man in the field had at some time or another experimented with the new invention, but in the majority of cases the experiment had apparently not been considered eminently satisfactory, as most of the cracks still remained faithful to the old gutty. There were one or two notable exceptions, however, and amongst these exceptions were the two finalists, Hutchings and Fry. Whether they realised that there must be an advantage in using the ball, or whether they found that it was a ball which was suited to their particular style of play, is a question for themselves to decide. I have an idea myself that they were wise in their generation, and readily appreciated a fact, which has since been so conclusively proved, that, whatever disadvantages were to be found in the use of this new ball, they were more than counterbalanced by the many advantages it conferred.

There was a general opinion at the time that the use of the rubber-cored ball tended to increase the element of chance in one's game. You might putt very well with it, and on the other hand you might go to pieces on the greens and lose all confidence. The play in the final round certainly tended to emphasise that opinion, as in the morning round nothing could have been finer than the short game of Hutchings, whilst in the afternoon round he exhibited the most evident signs of lack of confidence and hesitation on the greens. There may have been final rounds quite as exciting, and there may be again; but it seems hardly probable that ever again will a final be played in which a player more than once held a lead of eight holes, and then only scrambled home by holing quite a good putt on the very last green. The way those holes slipped away from him was most extraordinary. He did not seem to be playing badly; but, in contradistinction to his play in the morning, nothing would come off for him in this round. He kept taking just one too many at nearly every hole — a notable exception, and a more than useful exception too, being the sixteenth hole, when, after two magnificent shots, the second of which reached the green, he eventually holed out in four. Even after these two shots, however, he was once again in a tight corner, as he was very lazy with his long putt, and left himself a good three yards from the hole; that putt he had to get in to obtain a half, as Fry had already holed one considerably longer. It was a crucial moment, as failure would have left him only one up with two to play; moreover, there would have been the moral effect of having lost seven out of the last ten holes; six out of ten was quite bad enough as it was. This final effort of Sidney Fry's, even although it ended in failure, must always rank as one of the pluckiest efforts in the history of the game; for a player to get holes back at the rate he did, it is of course almost a *sine qua non* that his opponent should give him a good number of chances, but it is not always easy to take these chances when they occur.

That year, in the time between the Amateur and the Open Championship, also played at Hoylake, there was naturally an abnormal amount of discussion as to the merits of the rubber-cored ball. Hutchings and Fry had both used it, and in this there certainly seemed an indication that there might be a slight advantage in deserting the time-honoured gutty; but, with the true conservative spirit of the Briton, the majority of the leading players would have none of the American ball. The professionals in particular set their faces sternly against the innovation; and, notwithstanding the lesson taught by the result of the amateur event, it is a fact that a week before the event hardly a single player of note intended to use a rubber-cored ball in the championship. By degrees, however, a few threw over their allegiance to the gutty, and amongst this number was Sandy

Herd. He came down to play in that championship a contemptuous hater of all rubber-cored balls, and it wanted a very strong practical proof of their advantages to shake his belief. Fortunately for him he obtained the necessary evidence from Mr. John Ball, jun., who, playing against him with the hated foreign invention, made such a mess of poor Sandy that he was promptly converted, no doubt strongly against his will. Nevertheless converted he was, and he used the rubber-cored ball during that championship, and won it. Whether his success was mainly due to the use of the new ball is a mere matter of opinion; but there can be but little doubt that, until nearly the end of the final round, when he broke down in rather alarming fashion, he played with more confidence than he had done in any championship for some time past. I remember well meeting him when he came in from his first round, which I found out he had completed in 76. I was so struck by his appearance of satisfaction that I at once came to the conclusion that the new toy was much to his liking, and proceeded to back him to win outright, with very satisfactory results in the end. This championship was a peculiarly in and out affair. Firstly, Vardon made such strong play that it seemed as if no one could catch him; his first round of 72, with two balls out of bounds at the first hole, being a phenomenal performance. At the end of the first day's play he led by four strokes from Herd; but the morning round on the second day served to completely reverse the situation, as Herd accomplished a 73, Vardon requiring 80. The former then led by three strokes, and unless they both broke down badly no one else was in it. At the commencement of the final round Herd exhibited not the slightest sign of breaking down, as he holed out the first seven holes in an average of fours. Then he began to throw strokes away in handfuls, and when he teed off to the last hole his total was 76. His second shot to that hole was an "over at any cost" shot; he took a wooden club and the ball pitched nearly up to the pin and, racing

past, went hard against the wooden palings
beyond. He was probably a little lucky here,
for the ball finished in the pathway leading into
a garden, and he certainly had an easier shot
than if he had been tucked up in the long
grass against the woodwork. At the time there
was a question as to whether he had the right
to open the gateway leading into the garden,
so that he could obtain a free swing of the
club, but it was very rightly decided that the
gate must remain closed; he recovered well and
very nearly got a four; this made his total 81,
and left Vardon a 78 to tie and a 77 to win,
both scores well within his compass, and I have
no doubt that Sandy began to regret the strokes
he had thrown away. Vardon, however, was not
playing the game he had been on the first
day, and when the last hole came to be played
he was left with only a four to tie. His tee
shot was a good one, but he had an extraordinary piece of luck with his second, as it
pitched short of the bunker and hopped over.
It is said that he had heard of Herd's misfortune in going under the palings beyond the

hole, and being afraid of doing likewise, he spared the shot too much. Still this slice of luck availed him nothing, as his fourth shot, a putt apparently of anything between seven and nine feet, just slid round the edge of the hole. Harry as usual simply smiled, knowing full well however that it had cost him his chance of the championship. My own scoring in that championship provided a peculiar coincidence. When I won the championship in 1897 my total on the first day was 155, and on the second day 159, giving an aggregate total of 314. In the year 1902, my totals for the individual days were exactly the same, viz. 155 and 159, and naturally the aggregate total was the same. There the coincidence ended, as in place of being first I had to rest content with the position of seventh. I only wish that I had played as well in the amateur event as I did in the open.

CHAPTER XI

THE championship of 1903 had to be played at Muirfield. Now I did once manage to win a championship at Muirfield, and as I have said before, in consequence the view seems to have been held that the East Lothian course was one peculiarly suited to my style of play. I cannot say that I am in fact at all in love with Muirfield as a test of the game. As it turned out my career was a short one, for I fell by the way in round number two before H. W. Beveridge. It was a game in which I had only to thank myself for my defeat, as at the seventeenth hole I played a half-hearted, headless kind of shot from the bunker beyond the green. It happened thus: I stood in the position of being one up with two to play, but my tee shot to the seventeenth was far from a good one, and I had to force my approach out of the rough. The shot was well enough played; but, as is often the case when a ball has to be forced out of long grass, there was too much run upon it, and it trickled into the bunker beyond the hole. My opponent very obligingly did exactly the same thing, and when we came up to view the balls we found that my ball was lying quite clean on the sand, whilst his was in not at all a favourable position right under the face of the bunker. I had literally the choice of every stroke in the field of bunker play, as the ball was actually teed up. I am afraid I chose the wrong one, as I tried to cut right underneath the ball with a lofted mashie, and I very much succeeded, for I cut so much under it that I still left it in the hazard. I eventually lost that hole, and also the match on the nineteenth green. It was a species of error of judgment for which there was no excuse. I should have been out of the hazard at any cost, particularly as Beveridge was lying badly, and could hardly expect to get his ball near the hole. But it is easy to be wise after the event, and I thoroughly deserved the fate meted out to me.

Robert Maxwell won that championship, and on form deserved to win it; but he *did* have a squeak against Herman de Zoete in the pen-ultimate round, in which the match was won and lost on the nineteenth green. I do not think I ever remember seeing two players who showed such signs of having had enough of it, and the fervent remark, "Thank God that's over," from the champion to be, seemed to come right from the bottom of his soul. His oppo-nent acknowledged after the match that when he was putting on the final green he was in such a state of nervousness that he was not quite sure which end of his putter he was holding, and his efforts rather bore out this admission.

At this period of my reminiscences I think it will be wise to omit any reference to personal efforts in the open event; it is best to draw a veil over them, and I shall consequently do so.

I have always looked upon Harry Vardon's win at Prestwick in 1903 as just about the most wonderful in his career. That he was a very sick man at the time there can be no shadow of doubt, and it was a truly marvellous example of mental pluck that enabled him to finish those four rounds and win by no less than six strokes. Further, I have an idea that had he been at all pressed in the final round he would have won more easily than he did; he was playing on the safe side, and rightly so, for he was leading the field by no less than seven strokes with one round to go, and anything under 80 would almost for a certainty have still left him in first place.

CHAPTER XII

THE Amateur Championship of 1904 at Sandwich will always remain memorable for the success of the American invasion. The idea that the Yankees were at last going to take part in the championship was generally received with approval, but I hardly think that there was a single British golfer who anticipated that they had any chance of actually proving successful. We well knew that Walter Travis must be a good player, as he had done so many great things over the water; but we laid the flattering unction to our souls that the standard of American golf was not nearly on a par with that played in the old country; personally I still believe that assumption to be true, and I say this notwithstanding the comparative failure of our four professionals in the recent tour in

Mexico. However, in Walter Travis we struck a golfer with extraordinary powers of concentration, and a man who has taken the trouble to thoroughly master the science of the game. When such a player is in form, as Travis undoubtedly was that week, he must be a most difficult man to beat. It was not so much that he accomplished anything particularly brilliant, but he maintained such a uniform average of really good golf that the man who aspired to beat him would have to go all the way. After the event there were many who openly expressed the opinion that Travis was distinctly lucky, but no man won a championship yet who had any reason to complain of fortune. Sufficient for the day is the luck thereof. It is so easy to criticise a winner's performance; for instance, there are those who hold the opinion that Robb should have beaten him. Perhaps Robb takes this view himself, and it is quite possible that in reviewing the round he may be able to remember one or two happenings which had a very serious effect on the

P

trend of events.   Again, Harold Reade actually
stood two up with four to play, but allowed the
last four holes to go astray.   When a man has
held such a useful lead with only four holes to
play and then gets beaten, it would rather appear
that he must have thrown the match away;
but all credit belongs to Travis for grasping the
opportunities which Reade gave him, and indeed
it was in this respect that the American player
proved such a success at Sandwich.   Whether
he was up or down appeared to make little
difference to him, as he still played the same
accurate scientific game, and his steady imper-
turbability undoubtedly had an effect on the
play of his opponents.   From my own point of
view, I only once made the semblance of a fight
against him, and that was when I had pulled
him down from four up to two up at the
eleventh hole, and there seemed a slight chance
that I might make a match of it after all, particularly as he had pulled his tee shot going
to the twelfth hole.   I have not the slightest
doubt that he deliberately played that tee shot

to the left-hand side of the course, but when
he had hit it there seemed a grave doubt as to
whether he was not in the rough. As it happened, however, his ball was quite clear, and
taking advantage of this he played a beautiful
shot with some manner of wooden club, the ball
finishing within seven or eight feet of the hole.
My response was distinctly feeble, and it was
that second shot of his which went a very long
way to settle the match, for I candidly acknowledge that the accuracy of that stroke had a serious
effect upon me at the time. Hutchinson did not
play at all well against him in the penultimate
round. It may be that he was suffering from
the strain of the previous encounter against
Maxwell, or it may be that, like one or two
others, he was a little over anxious to beat the
stranger from the far-off land. Again, Black-
well never seemed to be playing a winning game
in the final. He certainly made a big effort
in the middle of the second round, and in
making it had the misfortune to run up against
some heart-breaking putting, but Travis was

on top all the while, and to my mind never looked like a loser. A great deal has been made of Travis's wonderful putting, and certainly it was of the sensational order on occasions, but as he kept it up right through the week it could not be classed in the category of "flukiness." The greens were so beautifully fine at Sandwich that they were all in favour of the confident, determined putter, as some of the professionals proved in the following week. The fact is, Travis took every advantage of the very favourable conditions. He had already gauged the strength of the greens to a nicety; all he had to do was to hit the ball truly, and it must go near the hole. In conclusion, I am not one of those who believe that there was the slightest element of luck in the success of Walter J. Travis at Sandwich in 1904. On the week's play he was the most consistent golfer in the field, and if his opponents did not play well against him there is a possibility that this very consistency had a deleterious effect on their play.

I always look upon the Open Championship of 1904 as supplying the most sensational golf in the history of that event. Certainly everything was in favour of the players, and the course was distinctly easier than when the amateurs had been competing in the previous week, as a great deal of the "rough" at the sides of the course had been shorn; still it was phenomenal golf, as is evidenced by the fact that there were no less than eight scores of 72 or under handed in, and the conditions of play on the first two days were not of the most ideal description. The pace on the last day was terrific. White began with a 72, but Braid easily eclipsed this with a 69, only to see this score beaten later in the day by Taylor, who got round in 68. Personally, I have always thought these performances phenomenal. It was generally anticipated that White, who was lying second to Braid at the conclusion of the third round, would break down in his final effort, and I heard more than one person express opinions to this effect. This was mainly of course on the score of temperament, as White has far from an ideal one for the game of golf. But on this occasion the critics were at fault, as except for a little shakiness in his driving towards the conclusion of the round, Jack White always had himself well under control. I was standing at the ninth hole when White arrived there, and found that he was out in 32; shortly after that Braid arrived at the same point in 34. He asked me one or two questions as to the score of some of the players, but he did not mention White's name at first, and I thought he was going on without inquiring; then just before driving off he remarked, " How is Jack White doing ? "   I answered, " Pretty well." " What's he out in ? "   " Thirty-two," I said. That made Jimmy look very serious, and when to a further query I replied that, as far as I could gather, White had started home with three fours, he looked more serious than ever. He made a great effort to catch White, and the way he played the fifteenth hole, when hard pressed, was a treat to see. I think that most players were very satisfied with a four to that hole, but Braid actually got a three, played absolutely perfectly. Braid might have tied with White had he not been under an erroneous opinion as to what he had to do; he thought that provided he holed the last hole in four he would tie, with the result that he played the hole carefully for the requisite four, hitting his approach firmly past the hole, and taking care to keep his approach putt dead. The spectators, who were aware of his position, could not understand why he did not hit the approach putt sufficiently hard to reach the hole. It afterwards appeared that Jimmy was under the impression that a four would suffice to tie with White, and he looked a sadly disappointed man when he was told that nothing over a three was of any avail to him, at least as regards first position.

Whilst White and Braid were apparently fighting out this duel, the majority seemed to have forgotten all about Taylor, and considering that he had to accomplish a round of 67 in order to tie, there seemed some justification for the assumption that the championship was over; but Taylor came very near to accomplishing this colossal feat, as he only took 68, and that without the aid of a particularly brilliant finish. It was a wonderful effort and quite typical of Taylor.

Where was Walter J. Travis in this championship? Well, to tell the truth, he failed to qualify for the second day's play; but those who regard this fact as showing that there must have been an element of flukiness in his win during the previous week, are probably not aware of the fact that the amateur champion only competed under compulsion, and I am certain from what I saw of his play that he did not care a button whether he returned a good score or not.

CHAPTER XIII

Never stop trying. It is easy to give this advice, but I know well that it is very difficult to follow, particularly when playing a medal round. How many times it has been driven home to me I should not like to say. Sometimes I have pulled an almost hopeless position out of the fire by sticking to my guns and trusting to the mistakes of others; but on other occasions I have thrown away excellent chances of winning simply by taking some rub of adverse fortune in a petulant spirit, and playing in consequence a succession of holes in a childish, casual manner. The Open Championship of 1898 was one lesson to me, as it conclusively proved that in such an event all is not lost, even if you do take eight to a hole only 160 yards in length. I kept myself well in hand that day, and in consequence I eventually found that, with six holes to play, no player held a better position than I did at that point.

In 1900 at Westward Ho, on the occasion of the Easter meeting, I had a double experience of the advantages of playing right through to the end of the round. In the first instance, I threw away a most excellent chance of winning the " Kashmir " Cup through becoming disgusted with my score. When play began there was a general opinion that two scores of just over 80 would have to be returned to stand any chance of success. But in arriving at this conclusion the prophets had somewhat under-estimated the difficulty of the putting greens, many of which had been covered by the tide, were in bad condition, and in consequence proved much more difficult than any one considered they would be. Going out I did not make at all good weather of it, and there was not much improvement for the first few holes home. Then I met a man who asked me how I was doing, and on telling him, he remarked, "Young Humphrey Ellis has got you all round the neck; he has two fives for 81." Promptly I began to slack, and eventually finished in 91. Great was my surprise when I came in and found out that Ellis had taken no less than eleven for the seventeenth, and had finished in 87, and even so his was the best card handed in.

In the afternoon round a mixture of bad luck and indifferent judgment at the first hole cost me an eight to that hole, and again I threw up the sponge for a hole or two. Eventually I lost to Mr. Horace Hutchinson by one stroke, and I do not think that any one was more surprised than he was winning with such a score. Now I am certain that had I stuck to my guns I could have saved a stroke or two, and I feel assured that there must have been several others in the field who could have done likewise had they only realised the possibility of such a high score winning. But the player has no one to blame but himself.

The useless regret, " Oh, had I but known," is of no avail. The chance has gone once and for ever.

This little experience in the contest for the " Kashmir " Cup proved a valuable lesson to me later in the meeting. In the final day of the meeting the scratch medal was open to visitors. The beginning of my round was simply appalling. The first six holes cost me no less than thirty-three strokes, and when I pulled my second shot to the seventh hole into a wilderness of rushes the situation appeared absolutely hopeless. When I found my ball it was not in any individual bunch of rushes, but there was only one way to play it, and that was to hook it off the toe of the club round a clump of rushes. A dangerous shot, but it had to be attempted, and I remember taking great care over the stroke. As it so happened, the shot came off, and I followed it up by running down a ten yard putt for a four. It was one of those extraordinary recoveries which do not come off more than once in twenty times.

From that point I could not do wrong, and I eventually won the medal by one stroke. I always remember that round principally on account of the fact that my partner was Johnnie Low, and by action and word of mouth he taught me much of the philosophical patience which is so necessary in the playing of the game of golf. He himself came sadly to grief at the same seventh hole, as he was unfortunate enough to place his second right in the heart of one of those clumps of rushes. How many he played there I cannot remember, but he played each succeeding shot more carefully than the other. Then after these many shots he considered the situation carefully, and concluded by picking his ball up and quietly putting it in his pocket. Not for one single moment did he exhibit the slightest sign of impatience or irritation, nor did he play his final shots without due deliberation. It was an object lesson in control which was not lost upon one individual present.

Time after time has this lesson of control

been driven home to me. To any player of an impatient or highly strung nature it is a difficult lesson to learn; but year by year it becomes easier to follow, for it is quite possible to school one's nature to a certain degree. I know more than one player who owes his success to the continuous schooling of an impatient temperament, and there is one professional, who has taken very high rank, who would certainly have not held the position he has done had he not realised the wisdom of developing by degrees a measure of philosophy quite foreign to his nature.

These two lessons I have quoted are far from being the only ones taught me during my career, but I mention them in this chapter as they prove such excellent examples of giving up and of holding on.

In the first case, one can see how easy it is to throw a chance away by not trying hard from start to finish, for one never knows that the other competitors may not be doing equally indifferently. The second instance is an excellent one of the value of the principle, "Never give up trying." By following it, you cannot possibly lose anything, and you may gain. More prizes and more matches have been thrown away through childish, peevish irritability than through any other cause. Watch the leading professionals. Occasionally they may be guilty of a slight lapse—they are only human after all—but it is seldom that they do not play the round through in the same careful manner, whether they are doing well or doing badly. They have learnt the valuable lesson of control, and learnt it through many years of experience. If we can learn a lesson from the professionals, so we can from some of the amateur exponents of the game, and I think that any one who saw Mr. Travis win at Sandwich and Mr. Barry at Prestwick would on close observation appreciate the full value of control.

TIGHT CORNERS

In a long golfing career every player must have been in one or two very tight corners; of course the tightness of the corner depends much upon the importance of the occasion. It may be that many a first-class player has saved himself from what looked like certain defeat by some *tour de force*, or through some egregious blunder on the part of his opponent, but these things occur more often in friendly matches than in the more serious events of the game. Well, I have got out of one or two very tight corners in private matches, but the worst I was ever in occurred in a game of not a little importance. It was in the Irish Championship at Portrush in 1902; I was playing against Johnny Bramston, and we were getting very near the end of the competition, as the occasion was the penultimate round.

To wander back a little, I may say that I had no reason to rail at fortune in reaching that round, as in the previous game I was two down with only three to play, but won the last three holes from my opponent, Harold Reade; but there was nothing ultra-sensational about the finish, as I had the best of every one of the last three holes.

It was a different case against Johnnie Bramston; to be quite truthful, I was a little outplayed, and found myself two down with six holes to play. I met further disaster at the long thirteenth hole, as after my opponent had played two indifferent shots I failed to find my ball. Eventually it was found snugly resting in a rabbit-hole. The ball had to be played where it lay. This seemed a moral impossibility, so I decided to carry it to the next tee. My feelings were more those of sorrow than of anger. At the fourteenth my approach was one of those which are termed "out of the box," just about four feet from the hole; but more trouble was to come, as my opponent laid me what appeared to be a dead stymie. On inspection, however, I found that

Q

the fall of the ground was very much in my
favour: so I played for this fall and the ball
just toppled into the hole. I had all the best
of the next hole, and was finally left with a four-
foot putt to win. I didn't do it. I absolutely
never went near it. This made me angry, and
my anger prompted me to have *a go* at the next
tee shot. I had driven the green against Reade,
and was going to have another attempt against
Bramston. And didn't I have *a go*. I nearly
dislocated my neck, and finished by hitting the
ball hard on the head. I was simply astounded,
as whatever my golfing faults may be, topping
is never one of them. I could not understand
it, and was left thinking in sorrowful wonder.
In the meanwhile I had not the faintest idea
where the ball had gone to. I simply knew
that it had careered along the ground. However I quickly received a rude awakening, as
a spectator audibly remarked, "Oh, he's hopeless,
he's in the gully, and Bramston has the whole
of Portrush to drive on to." This sounded
bad, as I had not noticed the gully before.

A respite came my way, however, as of all the portions of Portrush he had to drive upon he selected a dry river-bed on the right-hand side of the course. It was one of those extra careful shots which come to grief. I easily found my ball, as it was lying right in the middle of the gully, a very fortunate thing for me, for had it been a little closer to the bank it would have been almost an impossibility for me to recover. After a good deal of thought I played the shot and the ball scrambled out, but began to roll back again, until eventually a kindly bunch of grass arrested its progress. Then I had to play two more. The stance was a most uncomfortable one, one foot on a piece of ground in the clouds, the other on a more lowly portion of Ireland, and moreover I could not see the green. I brought the shot off all right, but overran the green some thirty yards.

Now came my adversary's turn. He played safe and chipped his ball out sideways, then played an approach on to the green, some eight yards from the hole. When I came to look at my approach I found that I could not possibly lay it dead, and had to rest content with leaving it five or six yards from the hole. Bramston laid his approach putt dead, and I was left with my five or six yards to save the game. It was not a nice one, as it was all round a corner. It was neck or nothing; however, it came off. Still the state of the game was dormie two against me, not a very happy position of affairs. To the seventeenth—a one-shot hole—my tee shot was far from good, but it cleared the bunker, and by some miraculous means received a very favourable kick towards the hole. I was quite unaware of this piece of good fortune until I arrived on the green and found the ball quite close to the pin. There was no time to inquire how the ball arrived there, as Johnnie Bramston had played a very good shot, and the situation was still serious. His approach putt was a difficult one, and he did not gauge it very cleverly; result, he left himself a putt of some eight or nine feet for a three. This putt he struck as true as steel; it seemed impossible that it could remain out of the hole, but by some miracle it did, and as I was dead in my second, I still managed to keep the match alive. The last hole was a curious one. The tee shots were quite good, and lying side by side; I had to play first, and as I often do when I am nervous, and I was nervous, I pulled my approach slightly. My opponent made a much more serious mistake, as he snatched at his stroke and hit it hard on the top; but it gaily hopped over the intervening bunker, and lay short of the green. His third shot was well played, and lay about two yards from the hole. The situation then was this. Two men distinctly feeling the strain —one six yards from the hole, the other man only two yards away. Man number one could save the match by holing his six-yard putt, and even if he missed there was a chance of man number two not holing his two-yarder. Still there were other things to consider, and one big "other thing" was the fact that that last green at Portrush is simplicity itself, in truth, almost as true as a billiard table. Now man number one — the author of this work — knew all about this, and came to the conclusion that unless his six-yarder went down he was lost. To hole a six-yard putt, even on the best of greens, it is absolutely necessary to hit the ball truly, and it is almost impossiole to hit a ball truly when, through the vagaries of the nervous system, the club is waving about like a ship in a gale. Could I keep that putter steady—not for any money. I kept addressing the ball time after time, but the club head would not come down quite where I wanted it to, and in order to pull myself together, I had recourse to the old subterfuge of " once again looking at the line." It was mere byplay, as I knew all about the putt, all it wanted was to hit the ball straight at the back of the hole. Finally I struck a happy moment, down went the putter right behind the ball, and it eventually disappeared into the hole. The nineteenth hole needs but little description. I cannot say that I played it well, but my opponent obligingly played it worse, and I won.

After the finish of this match there were two incidents which will ever remain engraved upon my memory. The first was a remark by an Irish golfer: " Well, you cannot have a nerve in your body; I never saw anything like it." He little knew what I had been through, and I didn't tell him.

The second was of a different nature. " Well, young man, you do play about with my money; please don't do it again." You see he had paid a very substantial sum for my chance in the selling sweepstake, and his money had certainly been in very great jeopardy; indeed, in looking back at that meeting I cannot help thinking that he was just a trifle lucky.

Printed by BALLANTYNE, HANSON & Co.
Edinburgh & London